CAR BUYING
R⬛⬛⬛ED

CAR BUYING REVEALED

ISBN10: 1-60037-400-X (Paperback)
ISBN13: 978-1-60037-400-5 (Paperback)
Library of Congress Control Number: 2007943362

Published by:
MORGAN · JAMES
THE ENTREPRENEURIAL PUBLISHER™
www.morganjamespublishing.com

Morgan James Publishing, LLC
1225 Franklin Ave Ste 32
Garden City, NY 11530-1693
Toll Free 800-485-4943
www.MorganJamesPublishing.com

Cover/Interior Design by:
Rachel Campbell
rachel@r2cdesign.com

Habitat for Humanity®
Peninsula
Building Partner

www.CarBuyingRevealed.com

DEDICATION

TO STEVEN, FOR GIVING ME the idea, my wife, for giving me the support, and my parents, for instilling in me the drive and courage to write this book.

TESTIMONIALS

USING *CAR BUYING REVEALED*, I had fun, yes fun for the first time every while researching and buying a new car! I felt empowered by your information and was able to make my deal happen over the phone which was unbelievable to me. I purchased a brand new Honda Odyssey Touring, fully loaded and saved at least $5087. Anyone looking to buy or lease a car has to use Car Buying Revealed!

JAMILA PAKSIMA

Exton, PA

Car Buying Revealed helped me purchase my Lexus ES 300 after having a difficult time at the dealer. I really wanted this car but the lack of courtesy and the games they played really put me off and soured my experience. Your expert advice helped me get the deal I wanted by helping me navigate my way through a tricky buying process. Car Buying Revealed is worth its weight in gold!

MICHAEL BRENT

Devon, PA

TABLE OF CONTENTS

X *Table of Contents*

FOREWORD

YOU ARE ABOUT TO LEARN EVERYTHING that car dealers don't want you to know. I am leveling the playing field so you are informed and empowered to get the fair deal you deserve. If you want to buy a car, new or used, without paying thousands of dollars too much, or being taken advantage of, you must read this book now and do what it says to do. This book will help you whether you are buying a car, a pickup truck, a minivan or an SUV. Too many people make mistakes when they buy a car and they don't even know it until it is way too late. I see it happen all the time. People spend thousands of dollars more than they should have when buying a new car. There are also a lot of people who think they are experts at buying cars and that they always can get a good deal. I'm going to show you how this is usually not the case and how to make sure you actually do get a great deal on every car you ever buy. I'll show you the most common mistakes made by consumers and how to avoid making these mistakes.

You will never get taken advantage of again when buying a new car, if you simply use the information in this book.

I have worked in the car business for over 10 years. I started at the bottom and worked my way into middle management which allowed me to work in almost all phases of the sales process. Not only will I tell you all the things you don't know, but I will tell you why car dealers do what they do and how you can use this information to get the best deal when you buy a car. I will give you all the tools and information you need prior to your next visit into a car dealership. Car dealerships spend a lot of money training their salesmen on how to make more profit from their customers, but nobody trains the customers on how to be a smarter buyer, until now.

A lot of people ask me why I wrote this book. It could be a long story that could fill another book, but here is the short version.

After spending 10 years in the car business I got out. I had reached the point of burnout and was sick and tired of working 70 hours a week and not spending time with my family. I missed too many family gatherings over the years and wanted them back. Once out, however, I realized that I was now on the outside looking in. I had to buy my own cars rather than have the dealer give me one to use as a demo unit. I didn't have the ability to know when the best deals were available. But when I sat down and thought about it, I really did have all the knowledge I needed to buy a car and get a good deal. I just needed to formulate a process and stick to it.

Then my friends started asking me to help them buy a car. They wanted to know the secrets for when they went to buy a car. I would explain it to them in a way that was insightful and organized. I would tell them how to wade through all the games that are played and how to handle themselves so they would get a good and fair deal. They were very grateful that I would share with them certain information that the dealers didn't want them to know. Then one friend made a comment to me one day. He said, "You should write a book on buying a car." I didn't think much of it until I met a publisher one day.

I was working part time as a limo driver and had picked up a customer at the airport. We were making conversation during our hour-long trip to his hotel and we got on the topic of books. We discussed our backgrounds, which included my years in the car business, when I learned that he was a publisher. After some conversation, he stopped and said, "You know, you should write a book on the car business." He came up with some incredible and brilliant ideas on how to write and market a book that would be helpful to every single person who would ever have to buy a car in their lifetime. He also told me that I could make a difference in thousands of people's lives by saving them tons of money whenever they went to buy a car. It was one of the most rewarding conversations I have ever had. Within a week I started to write this book. It was then that "Car Buying Revealed" was born, in the backseat of a limousine.

I have organized this book in the order of how you would buy a car. I have also made it easy to find whatever you need in the event you want to flip to different sections. Every chapter will have information that can help you no matter what stage of the car buying process you are in. The best way to get the greatest return from this book is to read it from cover to cover. I guarantee that once you do this, you will want to tell all of your friends about how much you learned from what I have shared. There are also several chapters of other helpful information towards the end of the book, as well as a glossary of terms that will be helpful to you. I have also included a list of recommended websites that you can reference for your research.

Buying a car is a bad investment. However, it is probably the second biggest investment that you may make next to your home. You are paying for a product that depreciates over the course of time. The problem is most people need a car so they can get to where they want to go. Because of that fact, you need to make sure that a bad investment is not costing you more than you need to spend. You need to keep your mistakes to a minimum and spend your money wisely. This book is your solution.

After reading this book, you should have the ability to buy your car over the phone, and be in and out of the dealership within an hour. Just by using the skills shared with you in this book.

chapter one
DOING YOUR HOMEWORK

you are about to learn everything that car dealers do not want you to know. I am leveling the playing field so you are informed and empowered to get the fair deal you deserve when buying a new car.

DETERMINE YOUR NEEDS AND WANTS

The first mistake people make when buying a car is that they don't know what they want. They let the salesman tell them what they want when all the salesman wants is a commission. The first thing you need to do before you buy a car is decide what your needs and wants are. Do you want a 2 door or 4 door? Automatic or manual transmission? 2 wheel drive or 4 wheel drive? Leather or cloth seats? The questions are endless but you need to decide what you need based upon how you will use the car. Do you spend a lot of time in your car? Do you need a lot of room for children, adults? Do you need to tow a trailer?

Take a moment and respond to the Table of Needs and Wants. Think about each item and determine if it is a need, want, both or you don't need it.

Table of Needs and Wants:	Need	Want	Both	Don't need
Automatic Transmission:				
Manual Transmission				
2 doors:				
4 doors:				
4WD				
2WD				
Leather Seats				
Cloth Seats				
Power windows/locks				
Color				
Capacity of passengers				
Gas mileage				
Insurance cost rating				
Safety rating				
Hybrid technology				
Safety rating				
Value retention				
Last more than 5 years				
Comfortable seats				
Sunroof				
CD/Tape player				
DVD player				
Towing capacity				
Storage capacity				

Power doors				
Keyless entry				
Navigation system				
Power seats				
ABS				
Side/rear airbags				

This list will help you determine what type of car that you need or want. Put all of your needs and wants together to see what car or truck would best fit them.

THE FOUR MAIN FACTORS TO LOOK AT WHEN BUYING A CAR

When buying a car, you should consider four main factors - quality, price, value and reliability. A car may have one or two factors but be missing the other two. You need to find a car that has all four factors. Foreign cars tend to be more likely to possess the four factors.

Quality is the workmanship and durability of a car over time. Many foreign cars, especially mid-size cars, can have a very long, useful life. There are many of these cars still on the road well after 100,000 miles of use. Domestic cars, on the other hand, tend not to last much past 100,000 miles even if cared for well. A foreign car will tend to be more durable and will have fewer problems than a domestic car with the same mileage. Consumer reports wrote that both Honda and Toyota were consistently better over time then the major domestic manufacturers. During a survey, they reported that Honda and Toyota were at least 55 problems per 100 vehicles better than the next closest competitor, Ford, which is considered to have an average amount of problems.

I once purchased a Toyota Camry that was 11 years old with 150,000 miles on it. It drove great. The heat and air conditioning worked great. It had a few glitches here and there but none of them affected my ability to drive or enjoy my car. I actually owned it for a long time and put several thousand miles on it with no major problems. If I owned a domestic sedan with the same age and miles, I don't believe that I would have had the same experience. Even today, if you look around while driving, you will notice a lot more older foreign cars on the road than domestic cars.

Price is not just the number on the window sticker. Price includes long term costs such as maintenance and repair bills. I have noticed that domestic cars may be a little cheaper than foreign cars on the average. But from my experience and others I have spoken to, it seems the long term costs of owning a domestic car are greater. They tend to have more problems down the line during the life of the car. I have also noticed that the cost of getting a domestic trade-in ready for sale on the lot is usually higher than getting a foreign car ready for sale. If you ask any mechanic, and I have asked probably over 100 of them, which type of car has better service histories, they all say that as a whole, foreign cars were usually better running and easier to maintain. They also added that domestic cars were easier to work on although they felt that a foreign car would hold up better over time.

Value is described as what your car will be worth over time. The easiest way to determine this is to look at resale values. The resale value and trade-in value of foreign cars generally hold up better over time than domestics. This has to do with quality and price which we just discussed. Another way to determine this is to look at lease programs. Foreign cars generally have higher residual percentages and therefore lease better than domestic cars. A Honda Accord leased for 3 years may have a residual value of 55% while a Chevrolet Impala comparably equipped and priced may have a residual value of 40%. Even the banks know there is a distinct difference in value over time. They are the ones that set the values. This is why more people lease foreign cars over domestics.

Reliability is the ability of a car not to break down over time. Sometimes it is referred to as dependability. Like we discussed earlier, mechanics tend to side with the foreign cars. Consumer Reports even claims that Asian vehicles are by far the most reliable in their latest subscriber survey. The vehicles in Consumer Reports are graded on a rating of problems per 100 vehicles. Asian vehicles have reported about 12 problems per 100 vehicles. European makes remained steady at 21 problems per 100 vehicles. As you can see they do not have the reliability ratings that Asian carmakers do. Oddly enough, in the same Consumer Reports subscriber survey, U.S. makes had an average problem rate of 18 problems per 100 vehicles. That was up from the previous year of 17. That is a better rating than the European models. Don't look at these numbers and think that all cars from a certain area of the world are the same. The results vary significantly within each group and should be researched more before purchasing a vehicle.

I owned an Audi Allroad for 2 years. It was a luxury European station wagon. It cost almost $50,000 but it had more warranty work done to it in that time than all other cars I have owned combined. This car was beautiful, fast and the safest car I have ever owned. I lost count of how many airbags it had. But it had almost $8000 in warranty work done to it. It was out of service for about 10 days over 2 years. Luckily, it was all covered under factory warranty and they also covered a replacement vehicle in the mean time. But the problem is that when you pay almost $50,000 for a vehicle, you think you are getting the best quality. That may not always be the case. I may have had bad luck, but it still seemed like a lot of work over the course of 2 years. I loved the car but hated the reliability. This is why reliability can be an important factor in deciding whether to buy a car whether it is foreign or domestic. Just because it costs a lot doesn't mean it is a reliable car. Not all cars have the same problem that I had. It just made me realize that paying more for a car does not mean you are always getting better quality or reliability.

I can't stress enough to do your research to find out if the car you want is reliable. The best place to start researching your car is at <u>www.ConsumerReports.com</u>. They are an unbiased report on all types of cars that show reliability ratings as well as more information that could help you decide on what type of car may work for you.

FOREIGN VS. DOMESTIC

Many people ask me whether it is better to buy a foreign or domestic car. This is a tricky question because all cars have a benefit to someone otherwise no one would buy them. I would start off by saying that foreign cars have come a long way over the years. Back in the 60's and 70's many Americans laughed at foreign automakers and said that nobody would ever buy a foreign car. Now, if you look at the biggest sellers of cars, you see the foreign automakers giving the domestic automakers a run for their money. Domestic sales are down while foreign sales are up. The "Big Three" of Ford, GM and Chrysler are no longer having an easy ride. Toyota, Honda and Nissan are biting at their heels. In fact, the top auto sales manufacturers for 2005 in order from top sales are General Motors, Ford, DaimlerChrysler, Toyota, Honda and Nissan. The interesting fact behind this list is that Toyota was only about 45,000 units behind DaimlerChrysler. In the car business, that is almost a dead heat. That number translates into about .3% of the total U.S. auto sales in 2005.

The amount of cars sold in the United States in 2005 was almost 17 million, which is about the same as 2004. In 2005, the Big Three Automakers sales were down 2% while the Asian brands' sales went up 7%. European brands actually fell by 3%. This shows that the Asian manufacturers are closing the gap and some are looking to be a new member of the Big Three. The challenge is to remain competitive in a very tight market. How they remain competitive is to build a car that has demand and is priced competitively.

The final sales figures for 2006 made everyone stand up and take notice. Toyota quickly snuck into the Big Three. Total sales were down from 2005 to 16.5 million new cars. But the interesting fact is the shift in market share. GM led the group with 24.65% of market share, Ford grabbed 17.26% of the market with Toyota right behind them at 15.41%. DaimlerChrysler was far behind the pack at 12.98%. They were 400,000 cars behind Toyota. Toyota has truly left their mark on the American consumer and they are only getting bigger and bigger. It appears to be a sign of things to come.

2006 was also a transitional year for all of the domestic manufacturers. For lack of a better term, they all appear to be in "crisis mode." Ford refinanced their debt to cut expenses, DaimlerChrysler sold off the very unprofitable Chrysler division, and GM seems to be going in circles. Union contracts are also up for renewal in 2007. The outcome of those negotiations will determine the future of the domestic automakers in the near future. Failure of the UAW (United Auto Workers) to accept some share of the costs of their employees may force the manufactures to send work out of the country where it is cheaper. Either way, the UAW may lose more jobs depending on what they want to give up and how much. This process will be watched closely by all as it will determine the economic climate and survivability for domestic automakers for years to come.

The domestic automakers have high expenses that impact profit margins. The cost to build a car for a domestic automaker is far higher than a foreign automaker. This is true for several reasons. First, domestic automakers use unionized labor. Unionized labor usually means higher wages and benefit costs. Second, the domestic automakers usually have high legacy costs. Legacy costs are the costs of supporting pension programs and the retired employees who are being paid a pension and have health benefits. With the constantly rising costs of health care, this expense is increasing drastically and impacting the expenses of the manufacturer. Third, domestic automakers have failed to keep up with market demand and adjust to customers needs. A perfect example of this is hybrid vehicles.

Toyota and Honda were some of the first to be successful at developing a cost effective hybrid vehicle to sell to the public. The domestic automakers did not take this seriously and figured that they would still hold the market on trucks and SUV's. What happened is that hybrid demand went through the roof and Honda and Toyota were ready for it and reaped the benefits. In 2000, about 9000 new hybrid vehicles were sold in the US. In 2005, almost 190,000 new hybrid vehicles were sold in the US. This is an increase in demand of over 2000% in 5 years. Honda and Toyota enjoyed this huge increase due to their hybrid sales accounting for over 169,000, or 89%, of the 190,000 hybrids sold in 2005. In 2006, there were over 246,000 hybrid vehicles sold in the U.S. 91% of them were sold by either Toyota or Honda.

The other automakers have some catching up to do in both sales and technology. Nissan finally came out with the Altima Hybrid in 2007, although they had to use Toyota's technology in order to make it happen. They could not come up with a good hybrid system fast enough to compete or be cost effective. Other automakers are also looking to lease Toyota's technology so they can jump into the hybrid market. It is going to be the wave of the future.

The domestic automakers were so far behind in the hybrid market that they had to catch up fast. They had to find a way to lure away the engineers from the other manufacturers. The only way to do this was to pay them a great deal more than they were already getting paid. By overpaying these engineers, the expenses of the domestic automakers went up as well. In other words, they had to pay a lot more for the same technology. Those expenses keep adding up and affect the domestic automakers' ability to be profitable. Later in this book there is a chapter on hybrid vehicles and how they compare to gas vehicles in terms or overall cost and alleged savings. You will be very surprised by what I found.

Foreign automakers don't have unionized workers so they have less expense when it comes to labor. They also don't have the huge legacy costs because they don't have the large amount of retirees that the Big Three has. For the foreign automakers who have implemented U.S. based manufacturing sites, they are relatively new to building their cars in the U.S., so relatively few employees have retired. They also put their U.S. factories in areas where the labor is cheaper than average. Places such as Ohio, Alabama, Mississippi, Tennessee and other areas of the country are where they can get high quality non-union labor. Many want to work for the foreign manufacturers because of their management style. They treat the employees better which leads to higher retention of employees. Employees that like their job work harder and take more pride in their work. This is where the foreign automakers started to surpass the domestic automakers in their quality of cars and ability to make a car faster, again for less expense. As with any product, the lower the expenses, the greater your ability is to be more profitable and competitive.

The foreign automakers also cut down on their shipping costs by building their cars here in the U.S. rather than overseas. Most of their cars are made here in the U.S. or just over the border in Canada. This allows them to be competitive by having shipping costs similar to the domestic automakers while getting their inventory to their dealers more quickly.

All of the domestic automakers are or will be having large layoffs over the next few years. Ford has announced that they are having 150,000 layoffs in 2007. All the executives are looking to take pay cuts in order to cut costs. This is a direct result of poor planning which leads to loss of market share and lower sales. On the other hand, the foreign automakers are hiring. The domestic manufacturing plants are operating at much less than 100% of capacity while the Asian automakers are generally running at 100% capacity or looking to build more factories to accommodate demand. This is an obvious sign of things to come in the car industry. You don't need to be an economist to see the trends that are happening.

I have worked for both foreign and domestic car dealerships. What I have noticed is that foreign cars are more popular and trusted over domestic cars. However, domestic cars are more popular when it comes to full size trucks and SUVs. There will always be a demand for these cars and the domestic manufacturers will always supply them. The problem is that there is a huge demand for sedans and smaller more affordable vehicles as well. This is where the foreign automakers have made their mark. They have made a car that is both high quality and reasonably priced. This is why foreign mid-size cars are much more popular than domestic mid-size sedans. Consumers have realized over time that the quality and resale value of a foreign car is generally better. This has also lead to better owner loyalty with foreign makes over domestics. Consumers who own a foreign car are more likely to buy the same make of car when they want to replace it. Foreign mid-size cars generally cost a little more than a domestic, but consumers feel that the added cost is well worth it due to the quality. A consumer may look at a foreign car that is comparable in price but may have more options than a domestic car. This added together with good safety ratings and a good resale value can make a decision easier for a consumer.

Domestic full size trucks are still in high demand. They have had some setbacks due to the fuel crisis but there will always be demand for them. Some consumers need these vehicles for either work or their need for a big vehicle at home to transport their family. Some people need them in order to satisfy their ego. Either way, there is a demand for them. The foreign automakers have made attempts to get into the full size vehicle market. Toyota has made the Tundra pickup in order to compete in the full size truck market and the Sequoia in order to compete in the full size SUV market. Nissan has the Titan full size pickup and the Armada full size SUV. People are buying them because of their great quality, but a lot of consumers don't use them for the function that full size trucks are designed for such as heavy work like snowplowing and heavy towing. As these trucks develop over time, you will see the manufacturers build these trucks in order do all the functions of domestic trucks. Other foreign automakers will also get into this market as well since they are slowly chipping away at the domestic market.

DEMO UNITS AND LEFTOVERS

Most dealers will put demo units and leftover vehicles in front of the showroom so people will be attracted to them. Demo units are demonstrator units that are used by managers to get to and from work. This is part of their benefit package. Demo cars usually have anywhere from 2000-6000 miles on them when the manager stops using it and switches to another demo car. The dealer then sells them as "demo units" which usually means that they are a little cheaper than a new car but it is still considered a new car and qualifies for all rebates, special financing and new car warranty. Keep in mind that the new car warranty starts at 0 miles, not the mileage of the car at the point you buy it.

Demo units are not always cheaper than a new car. Some manufacturers will give the dealer some type of incentive for using the car as a demo and then selling it. This helps the dealer sell the car cheaper than a new car by using the incentive to lower the sale price. The challenge is that not all manufacturers do this. Some dealers do not have the ability to price their demos better than a new car. The only way they can discount the price is to lose money on the sale of the car. If you are looking at a demo unit for a possible car to buy, make sure you look at a new car too. Eventually, if you don't want that demo, you may get as good of a deal on the new car as you would have on the demo that has 5000 miles on it. The dealer wants to sell the demo, but they won't lose the sale over you not wanting the demo unit.

Leftover vehicles are cars from the previous model year that are still on the lot. The manufacturers usually start sending out their new model year in the fall. For example, a 2009 model year car may show up in September or October of 2008. Once the 2009 models start arriving on the lot, the 2008 models are now considered to be leftovers. The manufacturer will not put good incentives on them at first but they will as more new models start to arrive. You will see them have special financing and big rebates until the end of the year and sometimes into the New Year. The rebates and incentives are even greater if the model was redesigned and the old style is a leftover. The manufacturer needs to make it worthwhile to a customer to buy a model that is already outdated. The downfall to buying a leftover is that your choice of cars will be somewhat limited as all the most popular colors and models will be the first to go. The least popular trim levels, option combinations and colors are left for last. If you are not as picky and are just looking for a good deal, then a leftover may be perfect for you. They do not always lease well, but you may be able to finance one with a good rate and some big rebates too.

Both of these types of cars, demos and leftovers, are something that you can get a good deal on, but you need to work a little harder to find one as they can be few and far between. It is not as easy as looking on a dealer website. They generally do not list demos on their inventory. You would only know when you go to the dealership and it is labeled that way.

WHAT YOU CAN AFFORD

Once you have decided on a car to purchase, you need to still do some more research. The first thing you want to do is find out more about the car that you want. The first place to look is your local newspapers to see what sales price is listed in advertisements. By doing this it can give you an idea of what your car will cost. It may not be your final cost but it is a good place to start. Keep in mind, all dealers will advertise a car that they can sell at the cheapest price. Generally, they will take the cheapest level of car and discount it as far as they can go. This is what is referred to as the "teaser" price. It is designed to get customers in the door so they can ask about this car but then find out that it is not the car they want or that it was "sold." This allows the salesperson to begin his "pitch."

If you look closely at these ads, they legally have to print at least one stock number on the ad to show that this car exists in order for this not to be considered false advertising. If a dealer advertises a monthly payment with this car then you need to look carefully at the fine print. These payments will sound good because they are actually a payment that figures in something such as a $5000 trade-in and a $5000 cash down payment with a 72 month payment loan, for example. These are also considered "teaser" payments. When these are advertised on the radio you will hear disclaimers at the end of the commercial by some guy who speaks really fast. The dealer is hoping that you do not pay attention to it. They want you to hear the good price and great payments so you will come in to try to get that deal. It is the classic "bait and switch."

Here is an example:

2008 Honda Odyssey starting at $399/month**

** Payments figured on sale price of $31,995, financing for 72 months @ 5.9% with $5000 cash down payment and $5000 trade-in. Payments based upon approved credit.

The ** would usually be found at the bottom of the advertisement in very small print. As you can see, it is a payment that is not readily attainable. It is designed to gain your attention. When a customer comes into the dealer and says "I saw your ad for $399 a month for the Odyssey," the salesperson will show them the car and then ask them "Do you plan on putting $5000 down and do you have a trade that could be worth $5000?" When they say "No," as most customers do, then the salesperson says "Well that is what that payment was based upon." Or he might say, "That payment was for another trim level than the one you are looking at," therefore the payment is higher. This process is the actual "bait and switch." The bait is the low payment for a nice car that brings you into the showroom while the switch is when they tell you that the payment was for a cheaper model. Then they "lead" you into a more expensive model that is more profitable for them.

There is another trick when it comes to advertising. What a dealer may try to do is make a used new car look new. How they do this is advertise a used car but make it look new by the way they word the ad. For example, using the example above, the ad may read something like "2008 Honda Odysseys as low as $22,995." Since a brand new 2008 Odyssey sells for $30,000 or more, this sounds like a great deal. The reality is that the Odyssey that is selling for $22,995 is a used 2008 model with 20,000 miles on it. The point of the ad is not necessarily to sell the used Odyssey, but to get people in the door for the new Odyssey. Conveniently, the "New" is left out of the ad except in the fine print.

The second thing that you need to do is determine what you can afford. If you are making a cash purchase, then determine how much you want to spend or can afford to spend. For most car buyers, some form of financing will be involved. To figure out your payment amount, figure how many months you want to pay (the term of the loan) and how much you want to put down as a down payment. There are payment calculators all over the internet that can help you figure out what your payment would be based upon the amount financed. Some can be found at www.MSN.com/loans or www.BankRate.com although I recommend the calculators at www.edmunds.com.

You should limit your loan term to 60 months. Any longer of a term is unwise. The reason for this is that your car will depreciate dramatically over time. The longer you pay the greater that chance that you will owe more than the car is worth. You are not paying it off as quickly so what will end up happening is that you will want to get rid of the car because you are either no longer interested in keeping it or need to get another one because your car is no longer running. What may happen is that you will go to trade in your car that is worth $500 - $1500 and you will still owe $3000 - $4000 on it. Now either this makes the replacement vehicle too costly because that money needs to be made up somewhere and would probably be rolled into the new loan or it just may not be feasible at all. The bank may not allow you to roll this into the new loan. This situation is much more likely as your term of the loan grows. This is why I recommend going no longer than 60 months on a car loan.

Your payment should also not exceed 20% of your net monthly income. That is, 20% of your total monthly income after taxes. Any more than that can affect your ability to pay other bills each month. If the car you are looking at is more per month on a 60 month loan than you budgeted for, then you may be looking at the wrong car. By the time you are done reading this book you will see why.

Occupation:	Annual Salary before taxes:	Monthly net income after taxes:	20% of monthly net income:	Amount Financed w/ 60 month term @ 5.9%
Retail salesperson	$ 16,000.00	$ 987.00	$ 197.40	$ 10,235.00
Waiter	$ 17,000.00	$ 1,048.00	$ 209.60	$ 10,868.00
School Teacher	$ 29,000.00	$ 1,788.00	$ 357.60	$ 18,542.00
Manager	$ 37,000.00	$ 2,282.00	$ 456.40	$ 23,664.00
Electrician	$ 49,000.00	$ 2,858.00	$ 571.60	$ 29,638.00
Police Officer	$ 52,000.00	$ 3,033.00	$ 606.60	$ 31,452.00
Sales Person	$ 95,000.00	$ 5,462.00	$1,092.40	$ 56,641.00
Vice President	$115,000.00	$ 6,612.00	$1,322.40	$ 68,567.00
Doctor	$195,000.00	$ 9,913.00	$1,982.60	$102,798.00
CEO	$300,000.00	$ 15,250.00	$3,050.00	$158,143.00

Source: Salary.com

Above are examples of average income levels of some common positions. It shows how the salary can be figured into the income after taxes (known as your "net" income). From that you can figure out what 20% of your monthly net income is. This is the high end of the amount of money you should spend monthly on your vehicle payment. This amount is not what you can spend on one car, but your total car payments from all the cars you own. It also shows how much that 20% will allow you to finance over 60 months (5 years) with no money down using an average finance rate of 5.9%. Your final rate will depend on your credit score which I will discuss later in this book. As you can see the higher the income, the more you can finance. Spending any more than 20% of your net income may cause you to not have enough money for other basic necessities of life.

When you look into the long-term costs of owning a car you need to include one very important item, car insurance. Most people are so preoccupied with the car they are buying that they forget to call their insurance company and get a quote on the car they are looking to buy. Depending on the car you are buying, your insurance costs could go up a great deal, especially if you are buying a new car. Generally speaking, the newer the car, the higher the insurance costs. These costs need to be figured into your monthly expense for your car. Add what you pay now for a car payment and car insurance together and that is your total cost of your car per month. If you pay your insurance every year then divide it by 12 in order to figure out a monthly cost. Compare it to what you are paying now to see if you can afford the jump in costs. For example, check out the surprising ranges in insurance costs in the following table.

Vehicle:	Quote #1:	Quote #2:	Quote #3:
2007 Chevrolet Aveo	$ 341.00	$ 518.00	$ 590.00
2007 Ford Five Hundred	$ 310.00	$ 439.00	$ 606.00
2007 Dodge Charger	$ 299.00	$ 601.00	$ 668.00
2007 Acura TL	$ 331.00	$ 569.00	$ 669.00
2007 Toyota Sienna	$ 377.00	$ 452.00	$ 510.00
2007 Nissan Titan	$ 486.00	$ 545.00	$ 626.00
2007 Chevrolet Suburban	$ 401.00	$ 501.00	$ 679.00

This table shows figures I found while comparing different vehicles with 3 different insurance companies. They are all 6 month premiums with the same average coverage of bodily injury coverage of $100,000 per person/$300,000 per occurrence, $50,000 of property damage coverage, $50,000 of medical benefit coverage, uninsured motorist limit of $100,000 per person/$300,000 per occurrence as well as $500 deductibles for both comprehensive and collision coverage. This coverage is an average coverage for your vehicle and is very close to the coverage required by banks or lease companies. It would also protect you in the case of a serious accident. Most people do not think about their insurance coverage until after they have a major accident and wished they had chosen different coverage.

The requirements for auto insurance do vary from state to state so make sure that you are not purchasing more insurance than you need. You should also keep in mind that there are four states in the United States that do not require a driver to have liability insurance on their car if it is not financed or leased. Those states are New Hampshire, South Carolina, Tennessee and Wisconsin. Even though they do not require insurance in those states does not mean that most people are uninsured in those states. Most people do not want to be held personally liable and make the right choice by purchasing car insurance. They would rather do that than risk losing everything they own after they are involved in an accident. Remember, an accident is not something you plan or can foresee in the future. Protect yourself with insurance before an accident comes around the corner and hits you.

As you can see by the figures in the insurance table, the quotes vary greatly even though they are for the same levels of coverage. This shows that you need to shop around for insurance quotes prior to buying your vehicle. Also, you can see in the table, just because your car is small does not necessarily mean it is cheaper to insure. Smaller cars may have less protection in the case of an accident which means that the chance of serious bodily injury may be greater. Therefore, if the chance of injury is greater, then the costs of medical expenses may be higher as well. This shows that when you are shopping for a car you should also check the cost to insure it as well. A high insurance cost can make certain cars a bad investment as it adds to the total cost of the car.

RESEARCH YOUR CAR

If you want to know what the dealership pays for their cars, you can go to www.edmunds.com for the best information. If you pick out the car you want on the website, they can tell you what the invoice price of a vehicle is. This is what people think the dealer pays for the car. Edmunds also shows you the average price of what people in your region are paying for the vehicle you selected. You need to be very careful when you choose your options because your numbers will not be correct if you do not check off the same options that are listed on the window sticker of the vehicle you are researching. If you have not seen the window sticker of the actual vehicle you are researching, then you can use websites to find this information. A lot of dealerships are putting the window sticker or an electronic list of options on their website when you search a vehicle on their inventory. Sometimes you can find this information on the manufacturer website. One very critical tip, you must make sure EVERY DETAIL is exactly the same for the car you want. For example, make sure your quotes are for the same car, with the same options, same trim level (i.e. LX, SE, DX, EX, CE, etc.), same engine and same option packages or accessories. If you look closely at a window sticker, each option package should have a code next to it. It is usually 3 digits, three letters, or more likely is a combination of both. For example, one package may be called "XM1" which may mean it is the XM radio package or "C01" may be a leather seat package. Each manufacturer is different so please be aware of any these codes listed on the window sticker. This could make the difference between getting a bad price on the wrong car and a good price on the right car.

Edmunds shows you the average price paid in your area for this vehicle which is not necessarily the price you should pay for this vehicle. Remember, this is an average price. Some paid more and some paid less. I am going to show you how to pay less. But having this information is a good start. Some cars can be purchased at invoice and some can be purchased above invoice. Some can even be purchased below invoice. Any car can be purchased for below invoice if the situation is right and you work hard at getting a good deal. The most common cars that are purchased at below invoice price are cars that are plentiful on dealership lots, leftover vehicles, low demand vehicles and cars that are not in season. These cars are not limited to these choices but they are your best bets for getting a good deal below invoice price.

HOLDBACK

You now know from your research what the invoice price is on the cars you are interested in. Most people think that invoice is what a dealer pays for his cars. However, there are a lot of other factors that go into what a dealer pays for their cars. The first one is called holdback. Holdback is a small amount of money, usually ranging from 2-3% of MSRP (**M**anufacturers **S**uggested **R**etail **P**rice) minus the shipping charges, which is held back by the factory and is paid to the dealer every quarter on each car sold. For example, if a vehicle has a base MSRP of $20,000 and has a 3% holdback, then the holdback on that vehicle is $600. The amount of holdback varies from manufacturer to manufacturer.

As you will see, most manufacturers have holdbacks. Take the invoice and subtract the holdback to find the starting price of the car. Most dealers do not talk about holdback and treat that money as their own and not to be shared with the customer. People often hear about holdback but seldom actually knew how much it is, until now.

These are my latest figures of what holdback consists of, by manufacturer:

Make	Holdback
Acura	3% of the Base MSRP
Audi	No holdback
BMW	No holdback
Buick	3% of the Total MSRP
Cadillac	3% of the Total MSRP
Chevrolet	3% of the Total MSRP
Chrysler	3% of the Total MSRP
Dodge	3% of the Total MSRP
Ford	3% of the Total MSRP
GMC	3% of the Total MSRP
Honda	3% of the Base MSRP
HUMMER	3% of the Total MSRP
Hyundai	2% of the Total Invoice
Infiniti	1% of the Base MSRP
Isuzu	3% of the Total MSRP
Jaguar	No Holdback
Jeep	3% of the Total MSRP
Kia	3% of the Base Invoice
Land Rover	No Holdback
Lexus	2% of the Base MSRP
Lincoln	2% of the Total MSRP
Mazda	2% of the Base MSRP
Mercedes-Benz	3% of the Total MSRP
Mercury	3% of the Total MSRP

MINI	No Holdback
Mitsubishi	2% of the Base MSRP
Nissan	2% of the Total Invoice
Pontiac	3% of the Total MSRP
Porsche	No Holdback
Saab	2.2% of the Base MSRP
Saturn	3% of the Total MSRP
Scion	No Holdback
Subaru	3% of the Total MSRP (Amount may differ in Northeastern U.S.)
Suzuki	3% of the Base MSRP
Toyota	2% of the Base MSRP (Amount may differ in Southern U.S.)
Volkswagen	2% of the Base MSRP
Volvo	1% of the Base MSRP

When calculating holdback, use the following guidelines. If a holdback is calculated from the:

- **Total MSRP:** consumers must include the MSRP price of all options before figuring the holdback.

- **Base MSRP:** consumers must figure the holdback before adding desired options.

- **Total Invoice:** consumers must include the invoice price of all options before figuring the holdback.

- **Base Invoice:** consumers must figure the holdback before adding desired options.

Source: Edmunds.com

Holdback actually started over 50 years ago when new car dealers, who were not known to be good money managers, did not budget any money to pay their quarterly taxes. They usually spent every dollar they made and by tax time had nothing. What they worked out was for the manufacturers to hold back a certain percentage of the price that they would be given every quarter. Thus when the taxes were due they could pay their taxes. It saved many car dealers because so many were failing due to tax foreclosures. Today this practice turns into profit for the dealer.

REBATES

Make sure you check the manufacturer's website to take advantage of all the rebates. A lot of cars have more than one rebate for which you may qualify. **I've had some customers that qualify for as many as 7 rebates on one particular model that totaled almost $8000.** Some people qualify for rebates that are not even made public. For example, a lot of manufacturers will give an extra rebate for active military personnel or "loyal" customers. For example, if you own a Ford and are buying another Ford, then Ford may give you another rebate of $500 or more because you are being "loyal" to them. This is how the manufacturer tries to keep customers from buying another line of car thus losing them forever.

You need to be watchful and diligent in keeping track of rebates for which you are eligible. **Dealers are known to keep some rebates from you and keep them as profit for the dealer.** They can do this because the dealers get reimbursed for the rebates by the manufacturer through an online system. They put in the rebates when the car is sold and the money shows up in the dealer's account. The manufacturer would only catch them during an audit. A standard audit entails a couple of people from the manufacturer coming into the dealership, pulling 10 deals from the files and seeing if they are all in check. If you sell a hundred or more cars a month, then checking 10 files every few months really is not a true test of integrity for the dealer. This allows the dealer to push the envelope and keep a rebate or two every once in a while in order to pad their profits. After all, most managers are paid on the bottom line of their department, **so they know that every dollar means money in their pocket.** If a dealer gets caught doing it on a regular basis, they may get a full audit which will be a big mess and an even bigger headache for the dealer. Unfortunately, the first few times a dealer is caught doing this, the manufacturer tends to do nothing more than a warning.

You can usually discover if a dealer is holding back rebates from you by going to a few different dealers and see what they give you for rebates. One dealer may offer you more rebates than another which should send up a red flag for you. This is actually a little system of checks and balances you can run with the dealerships. Some dealers honestly may not be as savvy at finding all the rebates for which you are eligible. There are different systems that dealers use. Some use a third party system while others stick to the manufacturer's system. GM has the worst system that I have ever used. It is unorganized and difficult to read. Ford has the best that I have used. Their "Vincent" system is great. You plug in the VIN and it gives you all the rebates for which the vehicle qualifies. It is virtually flawless as an operating system but rebates change daily so a rebate may be available today but not tomorrow.

If your dealer has a hard time keeping up with rebates this may be your opportunity to get yourself an extra rebate that otherwise you were not aware of or one that the dealer may try to hold back on in order to pad their profit margin. A lot of the rebates that dealers keep are rebates they find after the fact. When they get into the office, a good clerk will check the rebates as they are being entered into the computer and sometimes find one the sales manager missed. This is when they tend to keep the rebate money as their own profit.

Keep in mind that not all cars have rebates and not all manufacturers give out rebates. Rebates are put out on cars that the manufacturer knows the dealers need to move. **A car with high demand does not usually have rebates.** If people will buy it without a rebate, then there usually will not be one. It is a simple way of managing inventory. If dealers have a higher amount of inventory than they like to see on a certain model, then the rebates tend to go up. It also works if supply is lower than they like on a model. In this case the rebates go down.

> **Honda has never offered rebates for as long as I have known about them. Their philosophy is that they do not offer them nor do they ever offer 0% financing. I surmise Honda believes that offering a rebate would lessen the value or integrity of their product and make it no better than a domestic car which they believe is of inferior quality and value. The benefit for you is that when Honda does offer special financing such as 2.9% or 3.9% financing from time to time, you can take advantage of it without having to worry about the dealer playing any games with rebates. This is one less thing to worry about with the Honda product line.**

SHIPPING CHARGES AND DEALER INCENTIVES

There is a shipping charge from the manufacturer added to the price of each new car. This is a non-negotiable charge the dealer pays but it is not figured into the MSRP when calculating holdback. However, it is figured into the MSRP on the window sticker. This charge is non-negotiable and is set by the manufacturer. The charge ranges depending on the manufacturer and type of vehicle. It will be clearly printed right above the **"Total MSRP"** at the bottom of the window sticker. Shipping charges are not a means of profit for the dealer. It is a charge from the manufacturer to the dealer.

There are other factors that go into the final price as well. There is something called "dealer cash" or "marketing incentives" that the manufacturer will put out in order to assist the dealer in moving inventory. It is usually used on cars that are at the end of the model year or when the inventory of a certain model is too high and it needs to be moved. It works this way. The manufacturer notices that they have an overabundance of a certain model on their dealer lots. They need to help the dealers clear out their lots in order to make room for cars that are being delivered. The way they do this is to stimulate sales of that model. The manufacturer will then issue "dealer cash" or a "marketing incentive" on that model. It may be anywhere from $100 to as high as several thousand dollars. This allows the dealer to be more competitive against other manufacturers when trying to make deals and sell cars. The dealer can now price his cars lower than the competition which should allow him to sell more cars and clear out his lot of inventory. When you shop around, you may be able to get a piece, if not all, of this "dealer cash" taken off the price. Its intent is to allow the dealer to be more competitive. These incentives come out from time to time but are more popular at the end of a model year. You need to keep track of these at **www.Edmunds.com** which has good up to date information. **You are not out of line as a customer to ask for this incentive or part of it during the negotiation process.**

There are also advertising allowances that are figured into the price for the dealer. These do not fluctuate over time but are meant to assist the dealer in advertising their products. They can be used for newspaper, TV or other advertising expenses. These are generally not negotiable because these expenses are used by the dealer. But I have seen dealers give this money away, by discounting the purchase price, in order to steal a deal from another dealer.

When a dealer determines his cost on a vehicle, he starts at "invoice", then they have "net" which is invoice minus holdback, then they have "net net" which is net minus advertising, then lastly they have "triple net" which is "net net" minus any dealer cash or marketing allowances. So the definition of "dealer cost" can be considered "fuzzy math." It really moves around depending on how the dealer defines it.

Here is how it looks:

MSRP:	$25989	
Invoice price:	$22340	**Invoice**
3% Holdback:	$670	**Net = $21670**
Advertising Allowance:	$325	**Net Net = $21345**
Dealer allowance (cash):	$1000	**Triple Net = $20345**

In this example, "triple net" is the actual dead cost on a new vehicle. This what the dealership really paid for the vehicle.

FLOORPLAN

There are other ways that dealers make money as well. These ways are generally not known to the general public because they do not directly affect the cost of a car but they do affect the profitability of a dealership. People ask me "How do car dealers make money if they sell a car for below invoice price?" I am now going to answer this question.

Most dealers choose to "floorplan" their cars. Floorplan is basically a mortgage or credit line that they hold on their inventory. Dealers will usually borrow the money needed to have their inventory on the lot. This is a normal cost of doing business. The cars are paid off once they are sold. Then another car comes of the delivery truck and goes on the floorplan line. Many banks that hold the floorplan for a dealer offer the dealer 30 – 90 days of free floorplanning.

This means that during the first 30 to 90 days (depending on the agreement with the bank) the car is on the lot and in inventory, there is no interest paid on this car. If the car is sold and delivered prior to the 30 to 90 days being up, then the dealer is given a floorplan "credit." For example, if a car is on the lot for 20 days before it is sold and the dealer has 90 days of free floorplanning, then the dealer now has a credit of 70 days. The 70 days of floorplan credit is as good as cash. That 70 day credit goes back to the dealer at the end of the billing cycle. If a dealer manages his inventory well and turns the inventory fast, then the dealership may get a floorplan credit every billing cycle which turns out to be a big check for all the days of floorplan credits.

Here is how it works:

- Car A arrives on the lot on 1/1 and goes on the floorplan credit line with 60 day of free floorplan interest.

- Car A is sold on 1/21 and taken off the floorplan

- 60 days of free floorplan minus the 20 days the car was on the lot = 40 days of floorplan "credits."

Let's use the figure of $8 of interest for each day or "credit" the car is on the floorplan line. 40 days of credit would be worth $320. This would go back the dealer at the end of the billing cycle. A large dealer carrying anywhere from 1000-2000 cars on their lot can make a great deal of money this way by managing their inventory properly and efficiently.

A dealer that still has his inventory after the free floorplan time is up must pay interest every day that the car sits in the lot. This is an expense to the dealer if they do not manage their inventory well. This may sound confusing but well managed dealerships can make this system work well and make lots of profit on it. This is how the dealer can sell a car below cost and still make a profit. This is why dealers want to sell the car that has been on the lot longer over a newer one, and to deliver every car as fast as they can so they do not have to pay floorplan interest on the cars in their inventory.

Some dealers will advertise that they owe no money on their inventory and therefore they must have lower costs. That may be true, but if a dealer is running a credit on their floorplan each month, and another dealer does not have a floorplan to earn credits on, then wouldn't the dealer getting money back from the bank have a lower cost? So not owing money on a car while it sits at the dealer may sound like a good thing, but it may not be when you look into it. Not all dealers have floorplan credits. I have seen that the larger dealers who can turn their inventory quickly have been the best at it. On the other hand, some dealers that I have worked for have medium size inventories and manage them well and in turn get floorplan credits. It is all based upon on how well the dealership is operated and managed.

SUPPLY AND DEMAND

In order to get an idea of what cars have the best deal, you need to understand the supply and demand of your desired car. For example, each manufacturer has its "bread and butter" cars. These are cars that have the most demand and generally have the most supply as well. The manufacturer uses these cars to get their name and insignia out on the street. When people see a lot of a certain type of car, they tend to think it must be a good quality car since so many people are buying it. Honda's "bread and butter" cars are the Honda Accord and Civic.

Toyota has the Camry and Nissan has the Altima for example. These are cars that you can usually get a good deal on because supply is high and demand is steady. These cars bring the people into the dealership.

On the other hand, some cars have high demand and low supply. If you are looking for a hybrid vehicle, your chances of getting a good deal are very slim since the manufacturer keeps the demand high by keeping the supply low. These cars even have waiting lists at some dealerships. Others will even have an ADM (Additional Dealer Markup) on the window sticker - as if the profit at sticker price was not enough! The best way to determine supply and demand for a vehicle is to see what dealers have for inventory and at what price they are advertising them. If they are advertising a vehicle with no price in the paper or do not even advertise them at all, then they generally are higher demand vehicles. For example, if a dealer advertises that they have a particular model in stock but do not mention the sale price, then that vehicle is generally a high demand vehicle. Availability is more of a concern than the price is. That model is probably hard to find and they take orders on them in order to guarantee a future sale and not lose it to another dealer.

If you are looking for a Honda Accord LX 4dr Auto, then check each dealer's inventory online for that car. Then look how many of that model they have in relation to their total inventory. This will give you a quick way to determine supply of that vehicle. Generally speaking, the higher the supply then the lower the demand. Another trick is to look at the stock numbers that are usually shown on the website. They generally go in chronological order from when they came into inventory. The older the car, the more likely a dealer is willing to part with it at a lower price than one that came in 3 days ago. You may see something like "Stock #: H2341" or "Stock #: H3624." The first stock number is lower and will probably be the older car that they want to sell.

CREDIT REPORT

Before you step in the front door of a dealership, you should already have an idea of what your interest rate is going to be. In order to figure this out, you need to know what your credit situation is. The easiest and best way to find out is to get a copy of your credit report and find out your FICO (Fair Isaac Corporation) credit score. The Federal Government passed a law that allows consumers to get one free credit report a year. Under the Fair and Accurate Credit Transactions Act (FACT Act) consumers can request and obtain a free credit report once every 12 months from each of the three nationwide consumer credit reporting companies (TransUnion, Experian and Equifax). This can be obtained at www.freecreditreport.com. Once you get your credit report, look it over and look for any false or duplicate entries. If there are any errors then you should contact the credit bureaus by letter documenting the error and any proof you have so it can be removed and cleaned up. One error could make the difference between obtaining financing and being turned down.

The only problem with getting your free credit report is that it does not give you your credit score. You need to pay an additional fee for that service. You may not like having to pay that fee but it is worth it in order to find out what your score is, as that is a determining factor of your financing rate as well.

All three reports will may different information and have different scores because each institution reports to different bureaus. Creditors do not always report to all the bureaus each month. If there are any discrepancies that are negatively affecting your scores, contact the bureaus and have it fixed. Having a lower credit score could increase your interest rate and cause you to pay a lot more per month for your car. I will discuss how you can improve your credit score later in this book. Your credit score ranges from 300 to 850. But keep in mind that if your credit score is a 720 to 740 or higher, you should qualify for the best interest rates and any factory sponsored special interest rates. Obviously, the higher your credit score, the better. If you have a score of 600 or lower you are at great risk of being declined for a car loan. The important point here is that the dealer should not know more about your credit history or score than you do.

CHECKLIST

So here is a quick checklist of what you need to do before you go into the dealership:

1. Decide on what you need or want
   - 2 or 4 door
   - 2WD or 4WD
   - Color
   - Automatic or manual transmission
   - Leather or cloth
   - What are you using the car for?
   - What options do you need?

2. Credit Score

3. Get an idea of what your trade is worth (see chapter later in book)
   - Check the online sources
   - Check local paper to get approx. value

4. Find out what you can afford
   - Figure out your budget (monthly payment if you are financing)
   - Check out newspapers for pricing

- Check your credit scores
- Figure out a payment
- Check insurance costs
- Figure out a purchase price that you can afford

5. Do research on your vehicle that you want
   - Consumer Reports
   - Messageboards or blogs
   - Friends and family

6. Figure the car payment you can afford using the 20% rule

7. Car Insurance

8. Holdback

9. Dealer cash and Market Incentives

10. Advertising Allowances

chapter two
SHOW ME THE MONEY!

THE PROCESS OF BUYING

now you have enough information to go into the dealership and start the process of buying a car. You always want to start with your local dealer. He wants your business more than anyone. Nothing causes more pain for a car dealer, especially a local one, than driving around their own town and seeing their brand of cars with a competitor's sticker or license plate holder on it. This means he will most likely give you the best price with which to start shopping.

YOUR ARRIVAL AT THE LOT

When you first get to the dealership, park your trade-in out of sight if you have one. Park across the street or in the service area. You do not want your

35

salesman to know that you have a trade-in. This is part of the process of getting the most amount of money for your trade. Handling your trade-in will be discussed in a later chapter. However, trade-ins are something that should not be handled or even mentioned at the beginning of the car buying process. You may want to visit the first time with a friend, with your friends car so you can avoid the discussion altogether.

The first thing a salesman is going to look at is what you are driving. A person's car tells a lot about their personality and the salesman knows this. He will look at what you are wearing and try to size you up as you walk onto the lot. An experienced salesman will pick out a perspective customer based upon their car and how they are dressed. Salesmen also look at who you arrived with. Did you come with your Dad? Or your husband or wife? A friend? How are you dressed? Are you dressed like a slob? Did you dress very nicely or did you dress casually? They size you up immediately and then do what they call "cherry picking." This means that a good salesman will scope out everyone on the lot and approach the one that he feels will be the easiest sale, or the one with the least amount of issues to overcome. The salesman tries to pick the "cherry" out of all the people on the lot. Obviously, you can not judge a book by its cover, but it happens more times than not and hunches tend to be correct most of the time. So if you take one or more of these factors out of the equation, you may throw off the salesman and put yourself in a position of control. Most salesmen are lazy and they will try to take the easiest customer. They feel the easiest customer is the most uninformed. After reading this book you will be in control, not the salesman.

Ideally, you should dress casually. Do not over or under dress. Someone who is overdressed may not get the attention of a salesman as the salesman may not want to "match wits" with someone who is smarter or more sophisticated. To many salesmen this "matching wits" scenario equals too much work to close the deal. If you are underdressed, a salesman may not want to deal with you or show you much respect. They may think that you are someone who may not qualify for a car loan and therefore they do not want to waste their time with you.

If you bring your friend or relative with you then the salesman will work harder as they need to convince both of you to buy the car. This is not a bad thing. Your friend or relative may be a voice of reason for you, bringing you down to Earth and keeping you grounded when you get overly excited about a car. This way you do not make rash or poor decisions. A salesman is not necessarily afraid of this situation but be careful that they do not try to separate you in order to win you over and not ask the advice of your friend or relative. Common ways they may try to separate you are letting your friend or relative test drive a car that the salesperson may have noticed they like or recommending that you visit their waiting area as they have a TV, a couch and free hot coffee. They may try anything that may sound more interesting to you than helping out your friend.

"THE BUMP"

An average salesperson will usually meet you while you are checking out cars on the lot. He will introduce himself and ask in which vehicle you are most interested. Now most people think that this conversation is relatively harmless. Actually it is the start of the sales process and you may not even notice it. Here is a sample of how a well trained salesman should interact with a customer at this point (Remember, well trained today means being focused on the goals of selling lots of cars):

Salesman: "What car are you interested in?"

Customer: "A Toyota Camry."

S: "Do you have a trade in?"

C: "Yes, a 1999 Ford Taurus."

S: "How much do you owe on it?"

C: "About $5000."

S: "How much do you pay a month for that car?"

C: "About $275."

S: "And how much per month do you want to spend on your new car?"

C: "About $350."

S: "But if you found the car you really liked, what would you be willing to spend? $375, $400?"

C: "Yeah, $400 I guess."

What happened in this conversation is called the "bump." You were "bumped" before you even walked inside the door of the dealership. What the salesman did was determine: (a) what you owed on your trade-in, so he knows how much more you owe than it is worth, (b) how much equity you have in the trade and (c) how much you are paying now for a monthly payment. He has an idea what the trade-in is worth from past experience but ultimately the sales manager will determine the value. Yet now he has a starting point. Secondly, he got you to spend $50 per month more than you actually wanted to spend just by using some quick word phrases. So you are being sold already, without even knowing it. **With the payment bump he now knows that he has about $2700 more room to play with the numbers.** This $2700 is what $50 equates to in a standard 60 month loan payment.

Here is an example:

Loan Balance:	$21,200
Loan Interest Rate:	5.00%

Loan Term:	5 years
Number of Payments:	60
Monthly Loan Payment:	**$400.07**
Cumulative Payments:	$24,004.21
Total Interest Paid:	$2804.21

vs.

Loan Balance:	$18,500
Loan Interest Rate:	5.00%
Loan Term:	5 years
Number of Payments:	60
Monthly Loan Payment:	**$349.12**
Cumulative Payments:	$20,947.05
Total Interest Paid:	$2,447.05

You can see what the salesman has already done to you. He has caused you to spend almost $3000 more over the life of the loan before you even sit down to negotiate the price of the car. He already has you convinced, or at least has you well on your way to believing, you can spend $400 a month when you really only wanted to spend $350. This is why you should give up as little information as possible to the salesman. He does not need to know how much you want to spend for the car or how much you want to spend per month. Your research has already answered these questions for you. He doesn't need to know at this point. Any information you give him besides your name and what type of car that you want is more than the salesman needs to know. **Anything else you say will be used against you later during the negotiation process. More importantly, do not tell the salesman whether you are financing or paying cash.** Against popular belief, you do not get a better deal if you pay cash for a car. You may get a deal with your plumber, but not at the car dealership. You'll see why I say this when I get into financing later in the book.

At some dealerships, you may be asked to fill out a credit application right away. **Do not do this.** They do this to see how good or bad your credit rating is. How good or bad your credit is determines how they will treat you. If it is bad they will be more forceful with you and try to push you into a car. If it is good then they will let you decide what you want and not lead you around as much. A well trained business manager can look at your credit report and read it like a biography to see what your spending habits are. This will help the dealer try to get you to spend more money. So whatever you do, do not fill out a credit application. If they question you about your credit, you can answer "I'm aware of my credit. I'm not worried about it." This is a non-confrontational answer that doesn't need a follow up question or answer at this point. Credit will be an issue when you get to the financing. Only then would you allow them to see your credit report if you chose the finance with them. Credit and financing will be discussed in a later chapter since it is later in the process.

THE TEST DRIVE

Your next step is to take a test drive. You should never buy a car without test driving it first. You may love the way a car looks but if you hate the way it drives or feels, then it is not the car for you. A well trained salesman will go on your test drive with you. Your salesperson usually does this because their dealership's insurance company requires him to but more importantly because they are continuing the sales process. They usually have a preset route which they know well and therefore know how long it will take. During the test drive your salesperson will make light conversation listening for cues of what you would like to do next. They will then try to determine what type of personality you have so they know how to deal with you. The discussion may include questions such as how much you think your car is worth, how much you want to pay, if you have been shopping at other dealerships and whether this purchase has a chance of being completed today. They also see first hand whether you dislike the car or are very excited about it. It is always best to be more reserved about your interest in the car for negotiation purposes. It is also a good way for the salesperson to show you all the features of the car. By the end of the test drive, the salesperson should have all of their questions answered. But this is a point where you can be in control if you play it right.

This conversation will start building the relationship and trust between the salesperson and the customer. This makes it easier for the salesperson to deal with the customer throughout the process and leads the customer to think that the salesperson is looking out for the best interest of the customer. The problem is that the customer quite often does not realize that the salesperson is actually acting in the best interest of their own commission. **So be careful of what you say to him because he will remember it and use it to his advantage later.** He will also watch your actions and reactions to see if you are taking "mental ownership" of the car. This means you are already buying the car in your mind, so you could be "ripe" for the picking by the salesperson. Do not show any emotion or you will play right into the salesperson's hands.

In order to remain in control, here are some examples of what to say at the end of the test drive. As you are getting out of the car, or in response to the salesperson's question of "So, what do you think?" are: (a) "It was alright." (b) "OK." (c) "I don't know if I like the color" or (d) my personal favorite, "Eh." If you dislike the car then feel free to tell them so. That way you can find something that you like. You do not want to give any sign to the salesman that you like the car. He will build on your emotion and try to turn that emotion against you in order to pressure you into buying that car today before someone else does. If he feels that you are "on the fence" about buying the car, he may be more likely to hit you with the next ability that he has: Cutting the price.

Now you have decided that you like the car or not, and you decide whether to look at other cars, leave or move to the next step. If you like and want the car then you will go into the showroom and sit at a desk and start the process of buying the vehicle. If you do not like the car then do not be afraid to tell the salesperson. They hear it a lot and are used to it. They know that about 20-40% of people that enter a car dealership actually buy a vehicle.

If you have no urge to buy the car then tell the salesman the truth. "I really don't like this vehicle. I don't think it will satisfy my needs." or "It really isn't what I am looking for." These are non-confrontational statements that leave everyone on an amicable level. Thank him for his time and go on your way. However, there still may be a car on that lot that may satisfy your needs, so keep your mind and eyes open.

GETTING THE BEST PRICE

Before you even walk into the dealership to sit down, you should have already calculated the base cost of the car. We will use the invoice minus the holdback and any dealer cash or marketing allowances. This is where you draw the line for negotiation purposes. Not many dealers will sell a car for below their cost, so we will work up from there. There is no set amount above cost that you should feel safe with because as I said before, you must determine supply and demand first. If a car model has plenty of supply, then your chances of paying closer to cost are pretty good. If a model has plenty of demand but little supply, then your chances of paying close to cost are slim to none.

Example:

MSRP:	$25,000
Invoice:	$22,500
Holdback:	$750
Marketing Incentive:	$500
Dealer cost:	**$21,250***

*Rebates will come out after this and are not figured into the dealer cost.

Some say that 5% over dealer cost is a good deal, but some dealers will sell for less than 5% over dealer cost, especially if they are competing with another dealer for your business. Some cars will never be purchased for a price anywhere near this number. That would be due to either a low supply of a popular or newly designed vehicle or probably a special edition of a vehicle that has a very limited production by the factory. Most dealerships will make their money off of full-size trucks and Sport Utility Vehicles (SUVs). These vehicles are generally sold for well over "5% over cost" unless there are extenuating circumstances such as a fuel crisis, slow market, high inventory and seasonal demand changes. Your goal should be to purchase a car for the best price you can find. However, a low sales price is just the beginning. The other critical issues such as financing terms and leasing will be discussed later in this book.

You can use your research and see what the lowest advertised price is for the car you are seeking. You should be looking on the internet for advertised prices at dealers as well as advertised prices in the newspapers. Newspapers are the leading media source upon which dealers rely on the most since most of their advertising money goes towards it. They put as much information as possible in that advertising because it is intended to get you in the door. Once you are in the door, it is the salesperson's job to keep you there and sell you a car.

Now you can start the process of buying a car. You have your research completed and you are ready to deal. Keep in mind that if you reach a point in the process where you believe that you do not have enough information or if the salesman is making you feel uncomfortable, then step back and hold off on going further, until you have the information you need. **There is no rule that says you have to purchase the car if you have started the process with dealer.** Go home and research some more if you feel it is necessary. You are in control, not them! This lets them know, too, that you are a serious customer and that they need to give you a good deal if they want to earn your business. They will do everything in their power to get you to buy the car that day. **They know that every day that you are not buying from them, you could be buying from someone else.** The best way of staying in control is to have the ability to walk away. If the dealer does not have the car you are looking for, they will usually offer to get it for you. They do this by "swapping" it in from another dealer. The problem here is that some dealers will charge you a "locator fee" in order to offset the cost of going to get the car. The dealer will also not discount a car as much if he has to incur a cost by paying someone to go get a car for you. Try to buy one that is in stock that fits your needs and desires. If not, then try another dealer.

Now here comes the part where everyone makes their mistakes. You've decided on a car. You know what it costs the dealer and you've compiled the preliminary paperwork. After the salesman gets all of your information, he's going to ask you to make an offer. **Whatever you do, do not make an offer.** Let them make the first offer. **The unwritten rule is "whoever speaks first**

loses." If you make an offer and they come back and accept it, this means you probably could have offered less. So let them start the offers. A lot of times the salesman will come back with a number that is usually at or around MSRP. At this point, you will notice that I have not mentioned anything about your trade-in vehicle. They are going to ask you probably a few times if you have a trade-in. You will always tell them "No" because I am going to show you how you deal with the trade-in after the deal has been made.

The easiest way to get a price from the dealer is to be up front and firm. Tell your salesperson you expect them to give you their best price up front. Ask them for their best "Out the Door Price." Tell them you expect this to be their best price including any administrative fees. Do not be afraid to have all of your research paperwork in your hand. This will let them know that you are aware of what they own the car for and that you expect a good deal. Be honest and tell them you are shopping around. **You also need to tell them that if they give you the best price of all the dealerships you are visiting, you plan on purchasing from them.** You are not lying to them because you **will** buy from the dealership that gives you the best price. This is your goal. This way you have been upfront with the salesperson, you let them know you mean business and you will be verifying that this is a "good deal" by checking it against other dealers. If it truly is a "good deal" then you will be back to make the purchase.

The chances are good that the salesperson will tell you that this deal is "only good for today." Well, if it is good today, it will be good tomorrow. The only difference will occur if you are at the dealer on the last day of the month. Rebates change from month to month and the rebates may get better or worse the following month. The dealers do not know what the new rebates are going to be until the day the rebates go into effect. So your shopping process needs to start no later than a few days prior to the end of the month.

ADMINISTRATION FEES

Once you get your "best price" ask the salesperson for a copy of the worksheet showing the dealership's offer. Also ask the salesperson how much they charge for fees. Some call them "administration fees" while others may call them "processing fees" or "dealer fees." All dealers have them. They are added profit for the dealership. They will tell you that it covers the processing of paperwork and maybe some title paperwork. Title costs should be broken out separately as they are paid to the state, but all the other costs are not your responsibility. These fees range from just under $100 to several hundred dollars. **They are nothing more than profit for the dealer.**

These fees aren't usually questioned so the dealership looks at that as free money. You may not end up paying it by the end of the process but you do need to know what they are when you go from dealer to dealer. So make them write it out on the worksheet that they give you. If they won't give you a copy of the worksheet, then ask them to write it on the back of their business card. **Make sure they write it down so they don't claim later that you wrote down an incorrect number.** Also make sure that they break out all of the rebates they are applying to this price as well as any special financing that is available.

With special financing you need to pay special attention to what rebates would be given up in lieu of the special financing. For example, you may be eligible for a $1500 rebate OR 2.9% financing. And lastly, before you leave the dealership, ask the salesperson one last time if this is their best offer. If he stutters or doesn't say "yes" then he knows he can give you a better deal. **Give him another chance to give you another offer.** If he doesn't, then remember that for when you go back to him later. You can use that later to work him over for a better price. At this point, thank the salesperson for his time and leave the dealership.

They may even try to have a "closer" come in and try to get you to buy the car by enticing you with fancy words and numbers. Their job is to get a number out of you, the price at which you will buy and try to make the deal happen. If this happens just tell the truth. **"Right now I am looking for the best price from dealers, and I will buy from the best one. I'm not ready to buy today. Thank you."** This is the best way to be able to walk out of the dealership without being confrontational and still maintaining a good relationship with your salesperson.

CREATING COMPETITION

This next step is similar to what I just explained but is a little easier. You know what you want and you know who has the car that you want. You should go to at least 2 other dealers in your area and do the same process as before except now you just want their best price. Tell them you are shopping several dealers for the best price and you will buy from them if after your shopping you find them to have the best price. You should spend less time in the dealership each time from now on. **Whatever you do, do not tell the dealer what your best price is so far.** Their standard statement will be "Whatever it is, we'll beat it. So come on down." That sounds great until you get to the dealer and find out they can not beat the price and they start "strong-arm tactics" trying to force you to buy the car. So tell them, "I would simply like your best price or you will not have the opportunity to win my business." Make sure again that they give you a price and the administrative fees as well. This is very important when it comes to comparing offers from dealers.

Remember, you are the customer and you are in control. If a salesperson or sales manager gets mad or frustrated with you, it is because they are not in control of the situation and they are going to have to work for a sale. This is where the good salespeople earn their money. They stick with it and gain a customer from it, often a customer for life.

FINDING THE BEST DEAL

Now you have gained at least 3 quotes. At home, you can sit down and look at all the quotes and see which one is the best. When you look at the quotes you need to look at the total price from each dealership. This should take into account all rebates and should include all dealer fees as well. Here is where it can get tricky. **You need to decide, if you are financing, what deal is better for you.** You need to figure whether taking the rebate is better or worse than taking the special financing. Here is a sample of how a rebate can make a deal better or worse:

$20,000 financed after $2500 rebate:

Loan Balance:	$20,000
Loan Interest Rate:	5.00%
Loan Term:	5 years
Number of Payments:	60
Monthly Loan Payment:	**$377.42**
Cumulative Payments:	$22,645.52
Total Interest Paid:	$2645.52

$22,500 financed after not taking the rebate:

Loan Balance:	$22,500
Loan Interest Rate:	2.90%
Loan Term:	5 years

Number of Payments: 60

Monthly Loan Payment: **$403.30**

Cumulative Payments: $24,197.77

Total Interest Paid: $1697.77

In this situation it is better to take the rebate instead of the special financing. Not all situations will end up like this. Look at this example to see the difference:

$22,500 without taking the $2500 rebate:

Loan Balance: $22,500

Loan Interest Rate: 0.00%

Loan Term: 5 years

Number of Payments: 60

Monthly Loan Payment: **$375.00**

Cumulative Payments: $22,500

Total Interest Paid: $0.00

$20,000 after taking the $2500 rebate:

Loan Balance: $20,000

Loan Interest Rate: 5.00%

Loan Term: 5 years

Number of Payments: 60

Monthly Loan Payment: **$377.42**

Cumulative Payments: $22,645.52

Total Interest Paid: $2,645.52

In this case taking the special financing may be a good deal since the payment is lower. You need to figure this out each time you purchase a car because each situation is different and special financing varies from car to car. Some models don't even have special financing. **The dealer will always try to get you to take the rebate and use regular financing.** They make more money this way. But it may be better for you in the long run to take the rebate especially if you plan on paying the car off early or trading it in before you pay it off. This way you start with a lower balance. The savings only occurs when you take the loan to full term. If you are paying cash, then the decision is easy. Take the rebate.

0% FINANCING

People love the term "0% financing." It is like having a dream come true. Customers figure they can loan money from the bank without paying any interest and therefore afford a nicer car than they thought they could. This was true when it first came out after the 9/11 tragedy. The manufacturers threw this incentive out there to help keep the economy going. What they did not do early on was to give a large rebate in lieu of the financing. So 0% was taken advantage of by the customer every time. All the manufacturers' finance companies took a bath. They had a large amount loans with no interest coming in from customers. Then the manufacturers realized that they would be better off offering large rebates instead in order to convince customers to not always taking the 0% financing.

However, customers were still fascinated by the 0% financing and continued to take it even though the rebate allowed them to get a lower payment. This was actually a bad move for the customer. Instead of taking a $3500 rebate, they were taking the 0% financing. It all sounds well but keep in mind that now you would be financing $3500 more than you would if you didn't take the 0% financing. The problem here lies in the fact that you pay no interest on the car loan, but your amount financed is $3500 higher. Even if you want to pay the car off early, there is no savings. Usually if you pay off a car loan early or if you add extra money to your payment, your interest paid will be less because interest is based upon the balance of the loan. With 0% financing, you are paying the principal amount of the loan only each month, so there is no interest to be saved. And to make matters worse, your balance is higher from the start.

When you use traditional financing, paying extra each month will pay off the principal balance quicker than normal. This causes the interest to go down as well since interest is based upon the loan balance. With a rebate, your loan balance starts lower so you end up financing less. This may also help you in the event you have a total loss of your vehicle whether by theft, fire or accident. Your insurance company will only give you what your car is worth, not what you owe. So if you total your car, and you used the 0% financing, then you may end up owing the bank money when the insurance company does not completely pay off the loan. Your balance will be higher by a few thousand dollars than if you took the rebate and used regular financing. Having a lower balance and therefore having a lower risk over the course of your auto loan is the best reason for taking the rebate and using regular financing over 0% financing.

Also, be aware that another form of 0% financing exists. Up to this point, the only people who will offer 0% financing are the manufacturers' sponsored finance companies such as GMAC, Ford Motor Credit, Chrysler Financial and Toyota Motor Credit. Traditional banks such as Bank of America, Citizens Bank, JP Morgan Chase and Wachovia Bank do not offer 0% financing. They only offer traditional financing rates. The dealers know that customers will love to hear that only a dealer offers 0% financing. So they take a car which the manufacturer does not offer 0% financing and the dealer itself will offer 0% financing on the car. This one dealer that offers 0% financing on a car that other dealers do not can set itself apart from other dealers and generate a great deal of traffic.

I know this sounds confusing but here is how they do it. Let's say a dealer sells Toyotas. Toyota Motor Credit has not offered 0% financing on a certain model of car. So a dealer will "buy down" the rate. The dealer may get a customer to qualify for 5.9%. Then the dealer will "buy" the rate down to 0%, or whatever rate they choose, by prepaying the interest. If the interest on a loan at 5.9% is $3000, then the dealer needs to pay $3000 to the bank in order to get the rate down to 0%. How does the dealer get the $3000? They charge the customer for it by raising the price of the car. When they present the deal to the customer they will say, "This is the price that qualifies you for 0% financing." The customer does not always question it because they are just happy with the fact that they got 0% financing on their Toyota when no other Toyota dealers were offering 0% financing. You will pay more out of pocket when taking advantage of this special offer. Remember, anytime you see 0%, there is always a catch. Do not get caught up in the excitement of 0%. **0% sounds good at first but in reality it is not always a smart investment.**

DOWN PAYMENTS – THE GOOD, THE BAD AND THE UGLY...

A lot of people ask me how much they should put down when they buy a car. There is no concrete answer for this question. It really depends on your needs, wants and ability.

First of all, car financing is different then it was many years ago. Back then you were required to have a down payment in order to purchase a car. Now banks are less stringent on their requirements for financing. You do not need to put any money down on a car as long as you have decent credit or if you are not rolling a large amount of negative equity from a trade-in into the loan. The banks will loan you above the value of your car up to a certain point. This figure is generally 120 - 130% of MSRP or Invoice price depending on the bank. The dealers refer to his number as the "advance" that the bank will give you. As your credit declines in quality, so does the advance that the bank will loan you. You can roll the balance of your old loan into the new loan as long as it doesn't go over the bank's approved advance for that car. So the question is whether that is a good move to make.

The problem with putting no money down is that you now are pretty much guaranteed to owe more than the car is worth. Putting no money down does not help your situation. This causes customers to be in a bad situation. If your car is totaled in an accident, you may not get what you owe from the insurance company since they are only obligated to pay you what the car is worth. You also will not help your ability to trade this car in at a later date. You would have to wait until you have completely paid off the loan before you attempt to trade it in. If you are in this situation, then a substantial down payment may be in order. The down payment will obviously lower your payment and it will put you in a better situation if you need to trade the car in or if you are in an accident.

How much of a down payment in this situation is a tough call. In a perfect situation you should probably be able to pay off the negative balance on your trade-in plus about 20% of the value of the car you are buying. That amount can be pretty steep and most people may not have that type of money lying around. Sometimes the bank may require a down payment in this situation as well if their guidelines limit the loan advance on the car that you want to get. A lot of deals at the dealership will not be completed because of this problem. Sometimes people owe too much on their trade-in above and beyond what it is worth and have no money down. The dealer may help a little on his end by discounting the car more in order to get you closer to the advance, but ultimately the bank decides how much to allow you. Keep in mind too that when you roll your negative balance into a new loan, your payment can go up dramatically. This may put you into a much higher payment than you can afford and eventually end up causing to you to not afford the car any longer. Since you owe too much on it, you may not be able to get out if it.

A lot of times a dealer will ask you how much money are you putting down. Like I said earlier, do not give the salesman any more information than he needs. He does not need to know this. The reason being is that the more of a down payment you are putting down, the more he can charge you for the car and still make it look affordable after he throws your down payment or "contribution" into the picture. He may also try to sell you a car that has a lot of dealer added options because he can offset the cost of those options with your down payment. They may also use some of the down payment to offset the value in your trade to make it look better. They may use it against you by saying that you need to put down $2000 in order to reach the payment that you want. You may only need $1000 but they are using that extra $1000 in order to "stuff" the deal with an extended warranty or other products that the business manager may try to sell you in order to gain additional profit. So not all the money goes towards the car, but lines the dealerships pockets with additional products. There a lot of games to be played by the dealer with a down payment, the trick is to not allow them to do it by not disclosing your down payment to your salesman.

Ideally, in a perfect situation, 20% is a good amount to put down on a new car. The reason being is that 20% is around the value you will lose the minute your drive off of the lot. Depreciation will be relatively steady for the rest of the life of the car. With this much down you don't have to worry as much about owing more then the car is worth. That could be a problem if your car is ever totaled in an accident or if you want to trade it in down the road. Any down payment above 20% is also good as you never know what the value of your car will be down the road.

On a used car, at least 10% is a good amount. It is not as much as a new car because the majority of the depreciation was already suffered on a used car. The depreciation on a used car is relatively steady and not as dramatic as a new car. This will keep you in a good equity position from the start so you won't have to worry about owing more than the car is worth. Any down payment above and beyond 10% is also a step in the right direction.

COLLECTING YOUR INFORMATION

Ok, so let's go back to your kitchen table. Now you have at least 3 different price quotes for the car you want. The most time consuming part is done. Lay out all of your quotes in order from the best price to the highest. You need to make sure that you add in the administrative fees that the dealer adds to the price. Now your job is to try to get these prices down even lower. Most people will take the lowest price and call that dealer and see if they can go lower. The problem is that you have not given them a reason to beat it. You will probably be thought of as just making up a number to beat, and the dealer will not respond because a good salesperson will know from how you are asking him that he has the best price. **There is no reason to lie to a dealer in order to get a better price when you can get a better price by telling the truth.**

The best way to get a better price is to call the dealer who has the second best price. Tell them that you have an "Out the Door" offer of $$$$ from another dealer. This is an offer that includes the administrative fee. Tell them the real number because they will know if the number is outrageous. Give them the opportunity to beat the price of dealer #1. If they do, then great. Do the same with dealer #3 to see if they can beat it. If they can't, then we go to dealer #4, if there is one, and do the same. You should do this in rounds. You just had round 1, now we move on to round 2. Look at your notes and see who still has the best price. If original dealer #2 now has the best price, then we call dealer #1 and see if they can beat the price of dealer #2. We treat each round the same way until one of the dealers has no more profit to give up or the other dealer just gives up altogether. Do not be concerned if they say "That is my best price but it is only good today." Like I said before, **"If it is good today, it will be good tomorrow."** Dealers do not turn down buyers. They are in the business of selling cars, not keeping them. **You are not in this to make friends, just to get the best price.** This will allow you to do this. Remember, the more competitive the process, the harder the dealers will fight for your business and give you a good deal.

So here is how it looks:

	Dealer #1:	Dealer #2:	Dealer #3:
Sale Price:	$20,500	$20,700	$20,300
Admin Fee:	$200	$250	$450
Total Price:	**$20,700**	**$20,950**	**$20,750**

In this case, you can see that even though dealer #1 did not have the best sale price, they had the best total price due to the difference in administrative fees. This is why you need to look at the total deal rather than just the sale price. With this example, you would contact dealer #3 and tell them that you have a total "out the door price" of $20,700. Then you can ask them to beat this price - not match it, beat it. They should give you a better price. After this is done you should then call dealer #2 and tell them the best total price you have and ask them to beat it. If they both happen to beat dealer #1's price, then call dealer #1 and tell them what you have for a best price and give them the opportunity to beat it.

Keep your notes as you go so you can keep track of what they give you for prices. Don't be afraid to tell the dealer that another dealer (you don't have to name names) has a lower administration fee. They may be more competitive if they know that another dealer has lower fees. They may lower theirs to get the deal. Your notes need to be good in order to make this work. (See www. CarBuyingRevealed.com for the "Price Tracking" Worksheet for this exact purpose) You should do this until the dealers say they can not go any lower. They may say this at first but let them know that the dealer with the lowest out the door price will earn your business. **Getting the dealers to compete against each other is the best way to get the best price.**

By negotiating the price while including the administrative fees, you get the dealer to start to negotiate away a good chunk of this fee in order to remain competitive. Let the dealers compete over the fees too, as this is a pure profit generator for the dealer. If you ask the dealer why they charge the fees they do you will get a bunch of different answers. Some will say it pays for the cleaning of the car, a full tank of gas, processing the paperwork, preparing the car for delivery and preparing the title paperwork. **These are all excuses and fictitious reasons.** The cleaning of the car is the price of doing business - not the cost to the customer. A full tank of gas is paid for by the manufacturer and can usually be found on the window sticker. The processing of the paperwork really does not take that long and again is the price of doing business. It is not your responsibility to pay for this. Preparing the car for delivery or giving it a PDI (Pre-Delivery Inspection) is also paid for by the factory. They get paid for it to be done, so you should not have to incur the expense.

Title paperwork should be a separate charge from the administrative fees. This is a real cost that the dealer does incur because in most states the dealer must file for a new title on behalf of the customer. The problem is that the dealer should show this separate charge rather than include it in the administrative fees. I've seen some administrative fees as high as $800 and have heard of some that are even higher. Even if you had to pay for everything that I just mentioned, you will still have paid for it all several times over. This just goes to show another way the dealers try to maximize their profits. Do not be afraid to tell the dealer that you think the administrative fee is excessive and that you think that you should not have to pay it. The standard line from the salesperson is "Everyone pays it." Well, I guess everyone else did not realize they can negotiate this down too. This is why you will always get a better deal using this book. By the way, the salesperson generally does not pay this fee when they buy their car.

The process of getting the best price is simple, but requires the proper steps I have just outlined. This proven process however may take some time. Buying a car is something you should not do without thinking it through and making wise decisions. **You have a responsibility to you and your family to spend your money wisely.** The dealership has a responsibility to maximize their profit, as much profit as they can by any means possible. Do not feel bad about being forward or assertive with a salesperson, because if the tables were turned, they would do the exact same thing to you and not feel bad about it. They may try to make you feel guilty about affecting the salesperson's commission, but there is nothing to feel guilty about. He does not feel guilty about the big commission he made on the customer before or after you or the last person he took advantage of because they did not have the skills that you have after reading this book.

SEALING THE DEAL

When you finally reach the best price, which is basically the point at which the dealer will not go any lower, you need to contact the "winning" dealer. Make sure the deal is still good if you put a deposit on it that day. Remember, some dealers will tell you a price to get you in the door and then once you get there they will say "That car was sold" or "My manager made a mistake with the numbers." There are all types of excuses but these two are the most popular. To protect yourself, you should keep all of your dealer quotes in case you need to go to the #2 price if your #1 deal turns out not to be exactly what you thought it was. Sometimes if you are not able to get to the dealer right away, you may want to ask them to fax you a purchase and sale agreement that is signed by the manager. This way you can verify the numbers prior to going to the dealership; you can also resolve any differences and have something to verify the vehicle information (i.e. model, color VIN, etc.) and the numbers for when you get to the dealer. You want to make sure that the agreement he faxed you is the same one that you are going to sign.

Once you get to the dealership who gave you the lowest price, ask to see the car you were discussing and test drive it if you have not already. Once that is done you should ask to see a "Purchase and Sale Agreement." This can also be called a "Buyers Order." It will have the dealer's name, the description of the vehicle which will include the stock number, mileage, color, number of doors, transmission type, number of cylinders and VIN number. You should check all of these against the car you are actually buying. **Sometimes a dealer will switch cars on you to one that has been in his inventory longer because he wants to keep his inventory fresh. They also may switch it to a car that has less options so they can pocket the difference in price. Most importantly, check the numbers on the agreement.** They should match the numbers that you agreed upon. The bottom line should match your "out the door price" they gave you earlier.

The administrative fees may still be on the Purchase and Sale Agreement but since you were negotiating the bottom line price, these fees may have been offset in the actual sale price. However, if the "bottom line" numbers do not match, then bring it up to the salesperson. Let him know that he "made a mistake" in the numbers and they need to be fixed so they match the agreed upon price. **If they do not change them, then get up and walk out.** They will usually fix the numbers if you go to do this because they do not want to lose the deal. Having the ability to walk out keeps you in control of the situation. **Being able to walk away is the best way to stay in control when dealing with a car dealer.** (When you leave the dealership, the dealer no longer has any control of the situation.) Once you find the agreement to be correct, **make sure the sales manager signs it first.** This means that he has signed off on the deal, and it is a real price. Once you sign it you make a legal contract between you and the dealer. This is why it is called a "Purchase and Sale Agreement." They are agreeing to sell you a product and you are agreeing to purchase a product based on the agreed upon terms.

If you do not take the car right away, you will need to place a deposit on the car. If you put down a deposit on the vehicle, you need to check one thing. Look at the line of the agreement where they put the amount of the deposit. You would think this line would be labeled "Deposit." A deposit is something you give to someone to hold as a pledge towards a purchase of a product. It is given back if the purchase does not go through. Some dealers will label that line "Partial Payment." **This means that it is a partial payment towards the purchase of a car.** This payment is generally non-refundable. Every state has a different definition of a "deposit" and what you can legally do with it. Some states define a "partial payment" as something completely different than a deposit. Each state is different so be aware of this. If this is the case with your agreement, cross out "Partial Payment" and write in "Deposit" and have the manager initial it. This precaution is just in case the deal does not work out and you want to get your money back. Some cases go in front of a judge so you want to make sure your interests are protected. If you want the best protection for this then use a credit card for the deposit. This way you can dispute the charge if necessary through the credit card company. You should also research the laws in your state in regards to signed contracts and "Right of Rescission" laws. They vary greatly from state to state.

chapter three

HERE IS WHERE THE REAL FUN STARTS...

THE BUSINESS MANAGER

n ow you've completed the Purchase and Sale Agreement. You've followed my whole process and got the best deal. Or at least you think. This is when the games really begin. You actually have gone through the simple stuff so far. At this point, the self proclaimed "great car buyers" pound their chest and claim victory over the car dealer. **In reality, the next process is where guys like me made their great deal a really bad deal.** And it is all because they never realized all the other aspects of the purchase were still able to be negotiated and that several items can be "stuffed" into a deal without you even knowing.

Once you've signed the Purchase Agreement you will be escorted to the Finance Manager's Office. The Finance Manager can also be called the "F&I

Manager" which stands for Finance and Insurance since that used to be the only products he sold. But nowadays, in order to be politically correct or to change the negative stigma of the position, they are now called the "Business Manager." Regardless, they are all the same and do the same process. **Dealing with the Business Manager is where you need to be on your toes.** He is the one that can move numbers and figures around so fast that you will not even know what hit you. Everything up to this point is what the dealer calls "front end profit." Everything made after the sale in the finance office is called "back end profit." An easy way to look at it is "front end profit" is the profit made from the car itself. In other words, the difference between what the dealership owns the car for and what they sold it for. "Back end profit" is any profit made from anything else such as financing, extended warranties, insurance products or added accessories. The "back end profit" is derived from items that the Business Manager usually sells.

There are many ways a Business Manager can make profit from a customer. All of these ways will be discussed in this chapter. He is trained a lot more than a salesman and has generally been in the business for a while with many years experience as a salesman. So he knows what is going on in all aspects of the deal and he knows how to sell. The most amount of pressure in the dealership is usually on the Business Manager.

The reason is that the car business is now such a competitive business that dealers are willing to take a small profit on the sale of a car with the expectation that the **Business Manager will make the majority of the profit on the vehicle.** So he is expected by the upper management to produce month in and month out or risk losing his job as the dealership relies on that profit to be competitive and profitable. Unfortunately, the pressure can make the Business Manager use tactics that are less than honest in order to make his numbers look good and make a good commission check. They are paid commission on everything they sell so the more profit they make, the more they make in their paycheck.

A Business Manager's pay plan may vary from dealer to dealer, but it usually consists of a small salary with about 80% of their income coming from commissions. Do not let them ever tell you that they do not make money on these products. He is lying to you. A Business Manager can average anywhere from $500 - $4000 of profit per car depending on the type of car and how skilled the customer is in dealing with him. They are compensated very well by the dealer to make sure that profit is made in the Business Office. After reading this, you will be skilled in dealing with the Business Manager.

F&I CONTRIBUTIONS TO DEALERSHIP PROFITS

F&I's contribution declined slightly in 2005, but still represents close to half of total profits. Big incentives on the front-end made F&I profits even more critical. About half the decline in F&I share can be attributed to the decline in service contract sales.

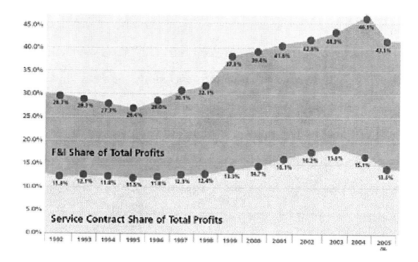

Source: CNW Marketing/Research

As you can see by this graph, the Business Manager (F&I Manager) is responsible for almost half of the dealership's profit each month. This is more prevalent in today's competitive market due to dealers making less profit on the sale (front end profit) of the car in order to remain competitive. In order to make this profit up they put the pressure on the Business Manager to sell more products on the "back end" of the deal. Since the pressure is so high on the Business Manager, they tend to take shortcuts or commit unscrupulous acts in order to make sure their goals are met and their commission checks are big.

The best way to counteract any of this mess is to be aware of what is going on and to be not afraid to ask any questions, especially if you don't understand what the Business Manager said to you. **Most importantly, do not let them answer your question with a question.** For example, if you ask the Business Manager "How much is my monthly payment?" and he replies with "How much can you afford per month?" then he is answering your question with a question. This particular question is very popular and the Business Manager is trying to find your limit or comfort level so they can adjust the deal accordingly. What they might do here is configure the deal with an extended warranty, life and disability insurance and an alarm system. They may also stretch your payment out to a longer term so it meets your "comfort level" for a payment. Then he will deliver it to you in a way that sounds appealing. Such as "Mr. Customer, I have some great news. How does this sound? I can get you the payment you want and I was able to also squeeze in some extra protection for you. You are now protected against anything going wrong with your car for 75,000 miles. If you are out of work due to an injury your payment will be made for you; if god forbid you lose your life your car will be paid off and go to whomever you chose to leave it to, and you will be protected from theft with an alarm system. How does that sound?!" He presented it in a way that builds excitement and gives all the benefits of the products he "stuffed" into the deal. What he didn't mention is that your finance term is now 72 months instead of 60 and your interest rate is 12%. Many customers fall into this trap every day but feel that the Business Manager "took care of them" because he was able to get those extra products for them at a reasonable payment. What they do not know is that some of the products would not be as useful to them and their payment without it was probably $50 less per month. **This customer walked into a bad deal all because they let the Business Manager answer a question with a question.**

If you want an extended warranty, then after you get the best price for your car you should also ask what price they will give you for a warranty. Tell them again that you will be shopping around for the best price on the warranty too. Nothing makes a dealer more worried than a customer telling them that they are going to shop their prices around. Have them break out the price of the warranty separate from the price of the car. Do the same with the other dealers.

Make sure you are aware of the type and brand of warranty that they are quoting you. Make sure you are comparing apples to apples when shopping around. If you get a price on a 6 yr./100,000 mile bumper to bumper manufacturer issued warranty then that is what you should request a price on at the competing dealers. Remember that manufacturer issued warranties are generally better as every dealer in the country recognizes them, but a lot of dealers sell third party warranties because of the increased profit margin. So, always ask who is issuing the extended warranty. Some dealers that sell third party warranties will sell you a manufacturer issued warranty if you demand it. Tell them that you will not buy the warranty unless it is from the manufacturer. Later in this book I will go over some reliable third party extended warranties that may work for you if you chose not to go with a manufacturer issued warranty. I will also expand on their benefits and how they differ in quality and service.

Once the process is completed the Business Manager will draw up the documents that you need to sign. These documents will be several pieces of paper that may include title paperwork, odometer statements, waivers, acknowledgements and finance paperwork. These are items that you should look at closely. Even if you are paying cash, you still need to look closely at the paperwork. The reason for this is that **there could be mistakes on the title paperwork that could be a nightmare to fix down the line once it is filed with the state.** Check your name, date of birth, address and any other personal information that may be needed. Of course, you need to check the numbers as well to make sure they match the numbers that were agreed upon and that they match the purchase and sale agreement. This may take a while so you may want to ask the Business Manager if you can see the paperwork prior to signing so you can take it to a desk and look it over without holding up any other customers.

One thing you will notice on a finance contract is your name at the top but more importantly right below that should be the **Federal Disclosure Box.** That box contains your interest rate, interest paid and total sale price as well as the payment and when it is due. Next to the payment should be the due date of the first payment. Most people expect it to be 30 days after the date of the contract. What a lot of Business Managers will do in order to close someone on buying one of his products is to offer them 45 days until their first payment. A month and a half to some people is very effective especially if they are taking on a payment that may be a little higher than they expected or wanted. Banks will allow the dealer to do that on every finance contract so that the dealer can push someone over the edge when they are debating on whether to purchase a car or a product in the Business Office. If I were a customer, I would ask to set my payment out 45 days every time. It makes your payment go up as much as

$1 but you should get what is rightfully yours. You don't have to buy anything extra in order to get this opportunity.

FINANCING (BANK OR CREDIT UNIONS?)

Earlier, I mentioned how you should find out your credit score if you plan on financing. This is to see what your credit situation is for when you get to this point. If you choose to finance, there are several things that you can do to make sure you still get the best deal. There is the situation whether you should choose a rebate over special financing. Those numbers were calculated earlier. Keep in mind that if you plan on trading your car in before your finance term is up or if you plan on paying it off earlier than the length of the finance term, then you should **always** take the rebate. You want your balance to be as low as possible. If there is a difference of $20 or less between taking the special financing or rebate, you should take the rebate if you can afford it.

You should also check your local banks and credit unions to see what their rates are. Most credit unions post their rates on their website. Most large national banks do not because their rates vary from state to state. Credit unions are also opening up their requirements for membership. You used to have to be an employee at a certain company to be a member but now sometimes you just have to live within a state or county in order to join. Each credit union is different. Most times you can join just by opening a savings account with $10. They should have the requirements for membership on their website. You want to check with credit unions first because they generally have some of the lowest rates around. Your local credit unions are definitely where you should start if you wish to finance your car. I advise that you start this process before looking for a car so you know what rate you would qualify for, and you can then see what payments you can afford. You should also know that some credit unions may not have the lowest rates but they are still the most competitive source for interest rates on car loans and are the best place to start.

You can do your financing at the credit union, other lending institutions, or you can do it at the dealership. I would generally recommend against using the dealership but they sometimes may have some better rates than your local credit union or banks have. If you want to take advantage of special factory sponsored interest rates or lease rates, then you must use the dealership for financing. The reason that the dealership may have better rates is that most of their contracts with local banks require the dealership to get better rates than the local banks give their customers that walk in the front door so they don't compete with each other. For example, if you walk into your local bank and they advertise a rate of 9% for a car loan, you may go into a dealer and use that same bank, but you may get a rate of 7%. The local banks really don't want customers going into the bank to finance their cars because the generally don't have the manpower to handle all of their customer's car loans. It takes a lot of work and time to do this and the bank feels that the cost of the manpower far outweighs the cost of maintaining that car loan. The bank actually makes more money when the dealership originates the loan for that bank and would prefer the dealership doing all the work.

Since credit unions are getting more popular, (there are over 9000 credit unions in the United States with over 87 million members) they have developed relationships with car dealers which allow the dealers to do the paperwork and originate the loan. This not only saves the credit union money in manpower but helps their customers take delivery of their car faster. The dealer makes a flat fee for doing the paperwork as they can not mark up the rate as they can with regular banks. Remember, credit unions are non-profit organizations that were instituted so members could take advantage of good rates and services that may not be offered by a bank or with the service of a bank.

There are several systems that these credit unions have joined so they can link up with the dealer in order to make this easier. One of the most popular systems out there is called Credit Union Direct Lending (www.cudirect.com). They provide direct lending by their credit unions through the dealer. It allows for "one stop shopping" by doing your banking and your purchasing at the dealer without having to make trips back and forth to the credit union.

HOW THE DEALER PROFITS FROM FINANCING

This is how the dealership makes money off of financing. It is actually very similar to the profit in a car, but it can be very lucrative for the dealer. Basically what happens is the dealer takes your application and shops it around to their banks to get the best rate. Once they get that rate, known as the "**buy rate**," they mark it up to a rate that they give to the customer, which is known as the "**sell rate**." How much they mark this rate up is up to the Business Manager and how much he can get the customer to take. This is where a lot of customers do not really question the rate because they are not aware of what the rates are in general, so they have nothing to compare it to. Most people do not know that the rate is negotiable. Therefore, they accept it and that great deal that they thought they had, now becomes a bad deal. Here is how it works:

This is what the dealer "buys" the money for on an average $20,000 car loan:

Principle Loan Balance: $20,000
Annual Interest Rate: 4.9%
Term: 5 years
Monthly Payment: 376.51
Total Interest: 2,590.54

This is what the dealer "sells" the money to the customer for:

Principle Loan Balance: $20,000
Annual Interest Rate: 6.9%
Term: 5 years
Monthly Payment: 395.08
Total Interest: 3,704.86

You can see the interest in bold. Notice the difference between the two numbers. That's $1114.32!!! This is the profit made on an average $20,000 car loan. The banks want this to happen because the dealer usually splits this $1114.32 with the bank. The average bank usually keeps around 25% of that profit and lets the dealer keep around 75% of it. So the banks are in on this too! They are also making money on this which is why they would rather you originate your financing with the dealer. This money that the dealer makes is called "**finance reserve.**" The greater the amount financed, the greater the reserve because the amount of interest is greater. This is why the dealer wants you to finance as much as possible. This is the most lucrative part of the finance process and dealers make a lot of money this way. This is why the dealer always wants you to finance with them because they want the opportunity to make more profit on you. This also is the easiest way for the dealer to make money from you because most people haven't done any research on financing. **They do plenty of research on the car but not enough or any on finance programs.**

This finance profit is limited by the banks. The markup on the rate is usually limited to a maximum of 2.5% to 4% markup depending on the rules of the bank. This does not apply to special financing which the finance companies do not allow except for certain rare circumstances. I know from experience that Audi Financial Services/Volkswagen Credit allows you to mark up special finance rates by as much as 2%.

The example above is a markup of only 2% which is an average markup. This profit gets even bigger when you go extended terms such as 72 or 84 months. Some banks will even go 96 months. That's 8 years! That's insane!!!!

Principle Loan Balance: $20,000
Annual Interest Rate: 5.9%
Term: 6 years (72 months)
Monthly Payment: 330.51
Total Interest: 3,797.04

Principle Loan Balance: $20,000
Annual Interest Rate: 7.9%
Term: 6 years (72 months)
Monthly Payment: 349.69
Total Interest: 5,177.61

Principle Loan Balance: $20,000
Annual Interest Rate: 6.9%
Term: 7 years (84 months)
Monthly Payment: 300.88
Total Interest: 5,273.66

Principle Loan Balance: $20,000	
Annual Interest Rate: 8.9%	
Term: 7 years (84 months)	
Monthly Payment: 320.77	
Total Interest: 6,944.47	

You can see the difference in interest when you go to what the banks consider to be "extended terms." The banks consider terms of 60 months or less to be "standard terms." Anything above those terms is considered "extended terms." Extended terms have higher rates as the term gets higher. That is because it is a higher risk to the bank. **A finance manager will always want you to go extended terms because he can make more money that way and you will have a lower payment.** As you can see from the 84 month (7 year) example, the dealership makes a $1670.81 profit which is more than $500 greater than if you did a 60 month term. That profit gets even bigger as the amount financed increases. The higher the balance, the higher the interest will be.

This is exactly why you should never tell a dealer that you are paying cash or that you already have outside financing. They count on this income from the financing in order to make profit on the car. If they know you are paying cash then they will not give you as good a deal because they know they will not have that "back end" profit that they count on. The same will be true if you tell them that you have your own financing. **If a dealer asks you if you are financing with them or not just tell them "We'll deal with that later. I am just looking for the best price."** This way nothing is disclosed and the salesman will take it as if you are financing and you are not lying to him. This simple statement should help you in getting the dealer to give you a price that would be lower than if you told them you were paying cash. This is why the dealer does not like it when you say "I'm paying cash." He knows his profit is limited when he hears that. Many customers have come into the dealer and the first thing they say is "I'm paying cash." As soon as they say that they have almost guaranteed themselves that they will not get a good deal. This is a common mistake committed by cash buyers.

Fortunately, this practice of finance reserve is under scrutiny in several states. The Attorney Generals are looking into it, and even legislators are getting involved to the extent that they are looking to pass laws limiting the reserve a dealer can make or that they need to disclose it on the contract. These "hidden profits" are why customers feel they are taken advantage of by a dealer. Many argue that this is something called discriminatory lending practices. Most consumers do not realize that they can negotiate the finance rate just like they negotiate the price of a car. What has been found over the years is that minorities and lower income consumers have paid a great deal more in finance reserve than the average consumer. Both GMAC and Nissan Motor Acceptance Corp. recently settled lawsuits over alleged discriminatory lending practices. I'm sure it is a matter of time when other finance companies suffer the same fate. **The old common way of conducting business is not an acceptable practice anymore, but until laws are passed, it will go on and you need to know about it.**

The scary thing is that the dealer makes profit on every customer that finances through them. That is why I recommend financing through your local credit union or bank if their rates are competitive. That will save you thousands in some instances. If you are willing to take on the challenge, you can see if the dealer can beat the rate of your bank or credit union. That does happen on occasion as rates do fluctuate regularly. You can get approved through your bank and then do an application through the dealer to see if they can beat it. The dealer will be more than happy to do this because once they control the financing, they control when the car is delivered and the chances of selling other products to you are greatly increased. Even if they give you the "buy rate" on your loan, they still get a flat fee from the bank that ranges from $100 to $300 depending on the amount financed. They won't make as much money off of you but you still need to be aware that the Business Manager can manipulate the numbers so you can easily get confused.

Some Business Managers will tell you that the bank did not approve you for the special financing but did approve you for financing at regular rates due to you having a low credit score. **Most times this is a story made up by the Business Manager so he can make more money off of you by marking up his rate.** Some special finance programs "tier" their rates. This means that as your credit score goes down, your special finance rate goes up. So instead of qualifying for 2.9% you may qualify for 3.9% or 4.9%. That is understandable, but once you are approved by a manufacturer for financing you should qualify for special financing which may save you thousands and not allow the Business Manager to take advantage of you. The best way to check to see if that is the case is to check the manufacturer's website and go to the financing section. This should break out the financing options available to you.

HOW THE BUSINESS MANAGER DOES HIS "SETUP"

If you decide to finance through the dealer, or even if you pay cash, you still have to go through the Finance Office. The Business Manager is still responsible for gathering the paperwork and putting it into the computer and printing the title work. He needs to make sure that your name and address are correct because if there are any issues with the title, it could be very difficult to fix after the fact. That is his primary function. He needs to get the car out the door as quickly as possible while still offering all of the services and products that he wants to sell you. He will move fast and try to find the easiest path to get you to buy his products.

Business Managers have very little time to spend with you in order to meet you and see what type of personality you have. He has about 30-60 seconds to determine your personality type. This will determine which pitch he will use on you. Sometimes, a well trained Business Manager will have a questionnaire for you to fill out before you get into his office. There will be questions such as whose name do you want on the vehicle title, who is your bank, who is your banker, how many miles a year do you drive your car, how would you make your payment in the event you were out of work, who would you want the car to go to in the event of your death and so on. All of these questions are geared to set you up for the products that he sells. This questionnaire is optional as you are not required to fill it out for any reason other than for his personal knowledge of your situation. **Do not fill it out.** Like I said, all that information will be used against you. All he needs for information is what is already on the Purchase and Sale Agreement. Do not give him any more information than he needs which are name, address and date of birth of all people on the title. Anything else he needs he can get from the application if you are financing through the dealership.

Every question the Business Manager gets you to answer is meant to help him with his "set up." A "set up" is when the Business Manager asks you a question where he already knows the answer. He uses that information to sell you products. For example, if he is asking you about your bank or if you know who your banker is, it is because it shows how your relationship is with your bank so he knows that you probably know what the current rates are so he needs to be cautious. On the other hand, if you don't know that information, then chances are that you are not aware of what rates are and he can set you up for a higher interest rate for more profit. He wants to know if there is someone else you want on the title in order to see if you are married or have a family so he can set you up for products such as life or disability insurance. He is setting you up again for life and disability insurance with the questions of how you would make your payments in the event that you were out of work or to whom you would like the vehicle left to in the event of your death. The question about how many miles you drive in a year is the easy set up for the selling of an extended warranty. If he does not do this in a questionnaire form, then he may just ask you these questions during his "interview" of you.

SALES PITCH

Now that all of his questions are answered he will pick his sales pitch to use based upon your answers. He will use one of two different methods of selling his products. It will usually be either "menu selling" or "straight selling."

The first and most popular technique is using a "menu." This is just like going to a restaurant and choosing a meal off the menu which comes with a salad and appetizer as well as a dessert. The products are grouped into usually 4 different choices that are grouped together. It usually starts with a choice that has all of the products, one with one or two products removed, then one with half or more products removed, and finally one with just the warranty included. Here is an example of a menu that you might see:

Customer Options
Mandatory Disclosure

Prepared for John Smith
Base Payment:
$250 @ 5.9% for 60 months
$200 @ 6.9% for 72 months

Amount Financed:
Sale Price:$20,000
Cash Down: $5000
Trade in: $5000
Total Financed: $13,500

Super Preferred Plan:

Extended Warranty
(6 yrs./100,000 miles)

Life and Disability Insurance

Tire Protection

Window Etching

LoJack Theft Recovery System
Gap Insurance

60 month payment: $302 ____
72 month payment: $251 ____

Preferred Plan:

Extended Warranty
(6 yrs./100,000 miles)

Life and Disability Insurance

Tire Protection

Window Etching

60 month payment: $295 ____
72 month payment: $246 ____

Standard Plan:

Extended Warranty
(6 yrs./100,000 miles)

Life and Disability Insurance

60 month payment: $280 ____
72 month payment: $230 ____

Basic Plan:

Extended Warranty
(6 yrs./100,000 miles)

60 month payment: $270 ____
72 month payment: $220 ____

By using this menu, it makes the choice for the customer look easier when in reality it can be quite confusing. First of all, all the important information such as the price and trade in figures are up in the right hand corner and the base payments are up in the left hand corner. These are the exact places where you really aren't looking because the menu is designed to bring your attention to the middle of the page where the important information is for the dealer.

This whole design was developed to make the customer have a more organized decision making process with little confusion. But in reality they are confusing. By looking at this menu, you think that the far right payments are your base payments. Also, by putting everything into packages and showing just a payment, it now makes it easier to sell a product because instead of saying "This product only costs $999," they can now say "By adding this product your payment only goes up $17. That's only about 56 cents a day." This is easier to justify in the customers mind. They liken it to buying a "value meal" at a fast food store.

If you look at the chart again you can see that your base 60 month payment is $250/month. But now, the way the menu is set up, it looks like you can have all the products in the "Preferred Plus" package for one more dollar a month. **The only problem is that the term now is 72 months.** Most people don't see that the term changes. All they see is that these products are good and they think "I can afford them." That's what makes this menu so lucrative to the Business Manager and the dealer. It is a way of selling more products in a non-confrontational way since the customer is making the decision without being forced into anything by the Business Manager. But this the trick. The Business Manager generally fails to mention what the base payments are without any products at all. **You think that you have to pick one of the choices when in reality you don't have to pick any at all.** They are just organized in a way that is easy to follow and a lot of these menus are colored so they keep your attention.

As a Business Manager myself, what I used to do is color each package a different color. The one that I really wanted them to pick because it fit their needs I would color green. The second one would be yellow and the third would be blue but I would never use red. Psychologically, red does not make people want to buy as they think of the word "Stop." Green of course has the opposite effect and makes them subliminally think that this is the right choice. Yellow is a soft color that they are not afraid of. So this menu is more than presenting information. It is a psychological ploy. It is all geared to get you to buy products. It also takes out the negotiation factor because many consumers feel that if it is in black and white on paper then it is not open to negotiation. **This is the farthest thing from the truth.**

Before you look at this menu, you need to ask the Business Manager what your base payment is and what your rate is as well as how much you are financing. Even though you know this prior to going into the Business Manager's office since you still have the purchase and sale agreement, you need to get him to tell you because this is where he starts juggling the numbers. Also, anything he offers you, he should be able to tell you the actual price. Don't let him ever say "it's only $$$ per month." **Demand the actual sale price of each product.** This will bring everyone into reality, whereas taking a sales price of a product and spreading it out over the course of 60 – 84 months does not seem as bad to the consumer. Seeing the real number might make you think twice about whether you need that product or not.

The reason this type of menu selling has become so popular is because it fulfills the requirement of "full disclosure." Full disclosure means that the dealer has disclosed all products that have been offered to you, and they also have disclosed to you what products you have purchased. The dealer is actually required to offer all of the products that you qualify for whether you like it or not. You may not like the fact you are offered a lot of products but the dealer is required to by the FTC (Federal Trade Commission). If not then they may expose themselves to a lawsuit. If they offer everyone an extended warranty but they do not offer one to you, and your car dies after the warranty period is up, then they may be liable for not offering a warranty to you. This is why many dealers are now making you sign a release that states you were offered these products but you either refused or accepted them. This is to cover all the requirements of full disclosure. The menu is a format where all the products are presented, which fulfills the obligation of offering every product to every customer.

All of these products mentioned can be found either on a menu, or sometimes they still will be pitched to you in a "straight selling format." Straight selling format is just when they try to sell you each product one at a time while going through each item and explaining them. It is very time consuming and not as effective for the Business Manager as far as time management. His job is to get you through his office as quickly as possible and on to the next customer. The menu allows him to do this quicker with less talking and less "selling." His intent is to go over the menu and tell you what is in each plan. He will watch you while he is going over the menu and see what your eyes gravitate toward and what you read over again to yourself. This tells him that you have interest in that product. After he's done going over it he'll ask you if you have any questions. If you ask about a product, then he will explain what it is and what it does. This is selling without actually selling. You are selling yourself.

Once you choose a plan, he will try to upgrade you to the next higher plan by telling you "it is only $$$ more per month to add this product." This makes it easier for you to justify the cost to yourself. Plus it would put more profit into the deal. Now there is something else you must watch out for. Once a plan is agreed upon, you will be asked to write your initials next to the payment to show you understand what you are choosing. If the payment on the menu says $251, it may be $250.62 but the menu system rounds to the nearest dollar. What can happen is when this is entered into the computer, the payment can be brought up to $251.89 by adding to the price of one of the products. **Since the menu only says $251 the customer has no idea what just happened and the**

Business Manager has gained himself more profit. If it is a 60 month loan then he has gained about $60 of profit in the deal. If he does this 100 times a month in a busy dealership, he can gain himself another $6000 in profit. Every little bit that can be added onto a deal will add up at the end of the month. Doing this every month can earn the Finance Department over $70,000 of profit a year or more.

This is why the Business Manager is so important; he can make profit appear without the customer even knowing it. He actually makes more profit from his products than salesman make on the sale of the car in a lot of dealerships. With dealers being more and more competitive in lean times, profit is always sacrificed in the front end of the car with the intent to be made up in the back end by the Business Manager. This is how dealers remain competitive and profitable in lean times.

PAYMENT PACKING

"Payment Packing" is another tactic used by Sales Managers and Business Managers. Either one may have given you a payment when you were with the salesman. You think that the payment that was given to you was the payment for the car only. What it really is can be called a "packed" payment. A "packed" payment is a payment that may already have a warranty, life and disability insurance and some other product or two added or "packed" into the payment. The Business Manager does this because if the customer likes the payment, great. The Business Manager's job is now easier. If not then you can remove products to get down to the payment that the customer can afford.

If the customer is sold on a payment and it is packed, then when they get into the Business Manager's office all he does is tell you that your payment is a "fully protected" payment. This is a pleasant description of what he has done. He will say that it includes "warranty protection for 100,000 miles, coverage if you are out of work or pass away or if you need maintenance. You don't have to worry about anything. If the car breaks down, or if you are out of work then your payment will be made and if you pass away during the life of the loan you will not burden your family with the loan balance, and they will get a free car and all of your oil changes are included. Nothing will come out of your pocket for the next five years except for gas. Isn't that great?!" This sounds good as he presents it. He says that you will pay nothing out of your pocket for these services. He is correct in that you will pay nothing down the road, but in the loan you paid $3000 for all of these products and added $60 to your monthly payment. **Basically, he put lipstick on a pig.** He made a bad deal sound great all because he presented it in a way that made everything sound like you needed it.

Some dishonest Business Managers will put products into the payment without the customer even being aware and without even telling them. This is dishonest, and it is sad that it even happens. It is usually done by Business Managers who are not very good and find that this is the only way to sell products. Not only is it dishonest, it is illegal in most states. He will usually try to get you to sign all the paperwork quickly without explaining them so you have no idea what he has just done to you. Now Business Managers are allowed a $5 window when they quote a payment in order to allow for fluctuations in interest rates or other factors such as registration costs or taxes. However, Business Managers have gone to jail for dishonest tactics and illegal activity all over the country. They push the envelope when they can get away with it. In one dealership alone in California, six employees were sent to jail, given probation and fined for this illegal practice. The saying in the business is **"Quote 'em an inflated monthly** payment, then peel 'em off the ceiling and see what sticks."** It is highly deceptive, and lawsuits have been brought about because of these methods.

Just because the Business Manager is offering products to you does not mean that the products are bad. But before you decide if any of these products work for you, you need to know what they are and what they do. There are several products that the dealer sells and all of them contain profit. Your job as a consumer is to keep that profit down as low as possible and allow the dealer a fair profit on the products that you do decide to purchase.

EXTENDED WARRANTIES

The first and most popular product sold by a dealer is the extended warranty. It is the easiest product to sell because most people understand the benefit to having one. It is one of the most lucrative profit makers for the dealer. I can not say that warranties are good or bad or that you should or should not buy one. That is a decision you need to make for yourself. What I can do to help with this decision is tell you the benefits of having one and how not to let the dealer take advantage of you when you purchase a warranty.

If you drive a lot of miles a year or you plan on owning your car for a lengthy period of time, then an extended warranty may work to your advantage. If during your research you find that the car that you are buying is prone to mechanical issues, then you may want an extended warranty to protect you against any failures in the future. If you plan on keeping your car for a few years and will not be out of the warranty period before you trade it in, or if you don't drive many miles per year, then a warranty might not be to your advantage.

There are several benefits to having an extended warranty. The most obvious one is that if your car breaks down after the expiration of the factory warranty, the warranty company will fix it. Another benefit is that on a lot of extended warranties there are other services that come with it that start from the day you purchased the vehicle. Services such as roadside assistance which can include lockout service, battery jumpstarts, fuel delivery if you run out, frozen locks, etc. may be included. Other services may include trip planning, rental car, emergency contact help and even trip interruption insurance. Trip planning helps you plan a trip by giving the best routes and any landmarks along the way. Trip interruption insurance would help you by giving you financial assistance for food and lodging if you break down a long way from home and the car is held overnight or for a few days. Some people get some of these services with a membership to AAA, while others have nothing. Rental car coverage is when the extended warranty will supply a rental car if your vehicle is in the shop for a minimum amount of time. Roadside assistance is also not included with every car make. The extended warranty may give you roadside assistance during the factory warranty as well since the manufacturer does not offer it with the standard factory warranty.

Keep in mind that the factory warranty coverage is whichever comes first, time or miles. If your car has a 3 yr./36,000 mile factory warranty, then if you drive 36,000 miles in 2 years, your warranty will expire on miles before your time is up. Keep that in mind when making your decision. Of course, the other side of the argument is if you never use the warranty, then that is money you spent for no reason at all. You gained no return on your investment. You need to weigh your options and see what a better investment is for you.

If you are interested in a warranty there are a few things you need to make sure of before you take the next step. The first thing you need to do is to determine what term and length you need. Warranties come in all shapes and sizes. There are 4 yr./50,000 mile warranties and there are 8 yr./100,000 mile warranties and several in between. You need to figure out how many miles a year you drive. The easiest way is to look at the car you drive and see how many miles you have on it and divide it by the length of time you have owned it. For example, if you have owned your car for 4 years and have 80,000 miles on it, then you drive about 20,000 miles a year. If you plan on keeping your car about 5 years then a 5 yr./100,000 mile warranty may be your best investment. Be sure you do not buy more time than you need and pay too much, or buy too few miles and not get your money's worth.

The second thing you need to do is determine who is issuing the warranty. Is it from the manufacturer or is it held by a third party? The manufacturer on most brands offers its own extended warranty. Some dealers will offer a "third party" warranty. This is a warranty that is held by a company other than the manufacturer. These are warranties that you should be cautious of. There are so many third party warranty companies that it is very tough to keep track of them. My experience tells me that the best warranties, if you are to purchase them, are from the manufacturer. They may be a little more expensive than a third party warranty, but the manufacturer will back them as long as they are in business and probably long after. Third party warranties can be from a less reputable company that is not financially backed well enough and may go out of business before your warranty runs out. **If this happens, you end up with nothing.**

There are very few "third party" warranties that I found in my experience that have been consistently good, from reliable companies with good coverage. The two most popular are Universal Underwriters and CNA. These two companies have been in the warranty business for several years. Universal Underwriters, which is now known as Zurich, has been involved in the auto business since 1922, and is still one of the largest warranty and insurance companies around. CNA has been around for over 100 years and is the 7th largest insurer in the

U.S. These companies are the only two that I have used over the years where I have consistently found their service and coverage to be excellent. The chances of these companies failing are extremely low. The service departments of dealers actually like these companies too for a couple of reasons.

First of all, they pay full retail prices for parts and labor for all work done to your vehicle. With manufacturers' warranties there is a set time and price they pay for each job which is less than retail. The dealer makes more money if you use CNA or Universal Underwriters. This obviously makes the service department more than happy to do the work. Second, the work is paid for generally with a credit card from the warranty company. This way the dealer gets paid immediately and does not have to worry about chasing the company for the money to pay for services rendered. Other third party warranties may not be accepted by other dealers or they may require you to go back to the dealer where you purchased the warranty if you are within a certain amount of miles of that dealer. Ultimately, the service manager just wants to make sure he gets paid for the work he has completed.

The level of coverage is what you have to be careful of when you buy a warranty. If you are going to buy a warranty you really should buy one that is as close to "bumper to bumper" as you can get. The reason is that a lot of the items that will break and be the most annoying are usually little things that are only covered under a bumper to bumper warranty. It also generally covers everything that the standard factory warranty covers.

Many Business Managers will try to sell a warranty, but will not tell you it is just a powertrain warranty. The reason is powertrain warranties are the cheapest warranty out there is because all they cover is the engine, transmission and drive axles. **They will sell the warranty to you at a bumper to bumper price and keep all the profit which can be in excess of $1000.** You will never know what level you have until you come in for a claim. The level is usually marked on the contract but most people do not check it. This is a practice in some dealers if the level of warranty is not explained or discussed. They will sneak it in if they feel they can make more profit this way.

To safeguard yourself, you should ask what level the warranty is. They usually have a brochure that explains what is covered and what is not. Keep in mind that no warranty covers "wear and tear" items. These are items that wear out over time and need to be replaced at the expense of the customer. These are items such as tires, brake pads, wheel rims, belts, oil changes, mufflers and exhaust system and cosmetic pieces such as interior items (seat covers, screw covers, etc.). Check the brochure or even better, ask to see a blank contract. The coverage should all be listed on the back.

Another thing to be aware of is the deductible on the warranty. A deductible is the amount that you as the consumer are responsible for when a claim is made. If the warranty repair costs $900, you will only be responsible for the deductible amount. Deductibles can range from $0 to $250 while some can even go as high as $500. **What a Business Manager may do is sell you the warranty at a $0 deductible price without ever discussing the deductible, and then when he draws up the paperwork he will adjust it to a $200 deductible which lowers his cost and therefore gives him more profit.** Business Managers tend to shy away from discussing deductibles just for this reason. They will also do the same thing with levels of coverage. You may think that you are getting a bumper to bumper warranty when in reality you got something between a powertrain and a bumper to bumper which will not cover the important and expensive items that need to be fixed. **This is a switch that the Business Manager can do so fast that you would never even know it happened.**

Keep in mind that if you buy a new car, you can usually still buy an extended warranty if you do so within at least 1 month or 1000 miles before the expiration of the factory warranty, whichever comes first. If you are not sure how many miles you drive or if you think your driving habits will change in the first three years, you may want to wait to purchase the extended warranty later because you can not change the term of the warranty once it has been sent to the warranty company. If you think that you may be moving closer or farther away from work, have relatives that are moving away or closer, or have a significant other that you may be visiting who is far away or even if your job location may be changing, then you may want to wait to purchase a warranty.

Another fact to keep in mind when making your decision is that you can get a refund on any unused portion of your warranty. For example, if you purchase a 6 yr./100,000 mile warranty and you trade the car in or it gets totaled in an accident at 75,000 miles and you have owned it for 4 years, then **you are entitled to a refund of your unused portion.** The warranty company will generally take whatever percentage you have used; in this case it is 75% of the miles but 67% of the time. They always take the higher amount of the two when figuring the refund. The higher amount used, the lower the percentage of your refund. So, in this case you would get back 25% of your original purchase price. You usually have to go back to the dealer where you purchased it with proof that the vehicle was traded in or totaled and proof of the mileage at the time of the loss. The dealer hates this because they have to refund a portion of their profit as well. Sometimes a dealer will try to hold back on giving back some of their profit as well. Do your own math when canceling the warranty to make sure you don't get taken advantage of by the dealer. Figure out what percentage you have used and then multiply it by what you paid for the warranty to see what is left. If you used 60% of the warranty, and you paid $1000 for it, then you should have $400 coming back to you.

So if you do buy an extended warranty, it may be better to buy a little more on the higher side of time and mileage if you are unsure of what you may need. Remember, it will run out on whichever comes first, time or mileage.

Here is another tip when buying a warranty. **If you purchase a warranty and then decide you do not want it, you usually have 30 days to cancel it and receive a full refund.** After the 30 days, the warranty company may prorate the refund depending on the mileage or time used. They may also charge you a cancellation fee. If you have financed your car and also your warranty, the refunded balance must go back to the bank. This is because they hold the first lien on the car and always get paid first. If you paid cash then it goes back to you. If you want to cancel it, you must do it well before the 30 days are up because **the dealer may "delay" your paperwork and cause you to go past 30 days and shortchange you on the refund.** They probably will also try to convince you not to cancel it because they have to refund their portion of the profit as well.

The extended warranty is the product that the dealer wants you to purchase the most. The extended warranty ties the customer to the dealership. Statistics show that a customer who buys a warranty is more likely to do their service at the dealership and they are more likely to buy their next car there if they have a good experience in the service department. The dealer will also get more business from that customer in warranty work as well. Therefore, the dealer needs this business so he can remain profitable and retain his customers and gain loyalty. This is why the Business Manager will push the sale of the warranty the most of any product on the menu. It is also the most profitable product as he tends to mark it up at least $500 from his cost. Sometimes they are marked up $1000 or more. Most people do not try to negotiate the warranty as they think "the price is the price." This could not be further from the truth. **Almost everything is negotiable in the business office. But it is where people negotiate the least.**

If you want to buy a warranty, you need to determine what you may need for time and miles and what level you feel comfortable with. Once that is determined, you handle this as a separate item. Once the dealer gives you his best price, you should say "How much would it be if I purchased a 6yr./100,000 mile bumper to bumper warranty." This makes it sound as if you are considering the purchase of a warranty. They may give you a price a little better than they usually give to help entice you into buying one. Once they come back and give you the number you should write it down and then say, "Is that your best price, because I'm going to compare it to other dealers as well." **If he says "Yes" right away, then he probably isn't telling the truth.** If he goes back to the Business or Sales Manager and then comes back with a better price, then you have obtained a lower price to start negotiating with later when you compare dealers against each other. You've already improved your situation.

LIFE AND DISABILITY INSURANCE

The second product that they try to sell you is life and disability insurance. This is generally a non-negotiable number since the rates are set by the state or the state insurance commission for that state. It is figured on the amount financed and the length of the loan. It can only be purchased if you are financing. Disability insurance makes your payments for you in the event you are out of work by a doctor's order due to a disabling injury whether it is work related or not. You usually have to be out of work anywhere from 14-30 days depending on the rules of the state in which you live. Life insurance would pay off the car in the event you pass away during the life of the loan. This portion is usually the cheaper of the two as the chances of you passing away are not as great as the chances of you being disabled. Keep in mind you can not get this insurance if you have an existing medical condition as outlined in the policy. You do not need to take a physical but you do need to fit within the rules. You can not already be out on disability when you purchase the policy as well.

Disability insurance usually covers only the first person on the loan but the life insurance can cover the first person or both people on the loan. If you have plenty of life insurance then life insurance may not be sensible for you. If you have very little or no life insurance, then it may be worth it to you. If you are single and have no assets or dependents then you do not need life insurance, as the bank can collect the car after you pass. It sounds cold, but it is reality. **The most important point here is -- Do not buy anything that does not have a benefit to you.** The dealer loves selling life and disability insurance because it allows them to finance more money and they can get up to 50% of the policy amount kicked back to them as profit from the insurance company. Unfortunately the opportunity to negotiate this price does not exist. If you are interested in this product then you should check with your car insurance company to see if they offer the same product and if they can give you a better price.

GAP INSURANCE

Gap Insurance is a somewhat new product. It is designed to protect the consumer in the event there is a total loss of your vehicle by theft, fire or accident and you end up owing more to the bank on your loan than the insurance company is willing to give you for it after your loss. For example, if your car is stolen and not recovered or if it is recovered and is deemed a total loss, and your insurance company is only giving you $10,000 for it, but you owe $12,500 then you have a deficiency, or a Gap. Gap insurance takes care of this difference plus your deductible on your insurance. This comes in handy if you traded a car in where you owed more than it was worth and financed the difference into the new loan with little or no money down. You never know when you might get into an accident, have your car stolen, or wreck your car resulting in a total loss. Plus you have little control of what your car will be worth over the course of time.

Markets fluctuate and what your car is worth will always go down over time. If you have put down a large amount of money, such as 20% or more in cash or trade, you probably have no need for Gap Insurance. If you put little or no money down and you did not roll any outstanding loans into this car loan, then it may be of value to you. Only you know your situation. Keep in mind that this does not cover you if you go to trade in your car and owe more than it is worth. It is only in the case of theft, fire or accident where there is a total loss of your vehicle. The policy itself can run from about $125 to $200 but the dealers tend to sell this for as much as $700. **This is also negotiable.** This can only be purchased if you finance your vehicle.

The type of Gap Insurance you purchase is important. First of all, determine who is backing the policy. If it is an established insurance company (Progressive, Nationwide, Allstate, State Farm, Liberty Mutual, Universal Underwriters, CNA) then you should be fine. If it is a holding company then you may want to be a little wary as with extended warranties - if they go under then you are stuck with nothing more than a piece of paper. Most Gap Insurance policies are backed by major insurance companies but some are not. Check the bottom or back of the form to see who holds the policy. If you have never heard of them, then be wary and research this.

The second thing to check on is the limitation of coverage. Some policies will only go up to 72 months. Usually on the front of the policy it will tell you how much it will cover in the event of a loss. This is usually something along the lines of 120% to 140% of retail value up to $50,000 or some variation of this. This example is an average coverage but some policies will have a stipulation that they will not cover any negative equity that was rolled into the loan. That means that if you traded in a car on this vehicle where you owed more than the trade-in was worth, and that balance was rolled into the new car loan, then that would be considered to be negative equity. In other words, if you traded in a car worth $5000, but you owed $7000 to the bank, and ended up rolling the $2000 difference into the new loan, then that is rolling your negative equity in to the new loan. This negative equity clause makes the policy useless because that protection was the point of buying it in the first place. If the policy says it does not cover it, and you are rolling a balance of another car loan into it, then ask for a different policy or do not buy it from the dealer. **Many car insurance companies will offer this coverage as a rider on your insurance policy.** It may be cheaper than what the dealer offers and serves the same purpose. Check the process and do the math to see which one is a better deal.

TIRE AND WHEEL PROTECTION

Tire and Wheel Protection is a program where if you blow out a tire, this program will replace or fix your tire and/or rim. It covers you if you hit a road hazard and either damage or destroy your tires and/or rims. A road hazard is something that is in the roadway that usually is not found there. These items are most likely potholes, pieces of metal, road debris, dead animals, car parts or any other item that is not found on public road. Curbs are usually not covered as they are permanently placed on the side of the road, therefore hitting one is considered an accident as it could have been avoided by staying on the travel portion of the roadway.

The companies that sell this product may be unreliable and a lot of dealers don't know how to process claims. They also may not cover you under some conditions or on certain types of tire damages. This is a product that I find to have little value or use because of all the "exceptions" that are generally found in the policy. It can cost anywhere from $75-$250 to the dealer, and they usually sell it for $299 to $599 or more. **Be wary of this product.** It may be worthwhile for people who live in an area with lots of potholes or road hazards, however.

WINDOW ETCHING

Window Etching is a product where the dealer etches the VIN number or another special code into certain windows or parts on the car to trace it back to you in the event it is stolen. **This is one of the most useless products you can buy.** First of all, do you really care if your car is stolen and they find your trunk lid in New Jersey and your hood in California with your VIN number etched in it? You care about the condition of your car when they recover it. Most people do not want their car back once it is stolen. Plus it only helps law enforcement trace your parts. Most police officers do not even look for etching when they recover a stolen car. They usually just call a tow truck and have it towed to the storage yard. This may give you insurance discounts in some states but usually it is not enough to offset the cost of it. The dealers who do it themselves may pay $15 for it and sell it for several hundred.

PAINT AND FABRIC PROTECTION

Paint and fabric protection is another product that dealers have been selling for years. The dealer slang for it is "rust and dust." This also is a product that has very little value. **Believe it or not, many times the dealer forgets to put it on.** Then they keep all the profit and the customer gets nothing. The way cars are made nowadays, they have more rust protection built into the steel and paint than ever before. They do not need anymore protection. If you feel it has value then you can buy it at an automotive store for usually 10% of what the dealer charges. The other problem is that if you want your car to be truly protected, you need to reapply the products every 6 months or so. It is more work than what it is worth. The best way to protect your car is to keep it clean by washing it regularly. If you live in the Northern part of the country then you should wash it regularly to keep the road salt from building up under the car which makes your car rust prematurely.

Your new car probably comes with a rust-through warranty, but only in the case of a perforation or a hole in the metal, not rust in general. Keep this in mind when taking care of your car. Also, not driving your car near the ocean will help keep your car or truck from rusting. It may sound weird to some people but believe it or not, some people drive their vehicles on the beach and get salt water in the undercarriage of the car and wonder why it rusts so fast. Wash it as soon as you get off the beach for the best protection of your vehicle. Some people who live by the beach may also drive through ocean water on their streets during large storms. This can also be tough on your car exterior over time. If you live by the ocean, then washing your car regularly may be a wise investment.

There is only one product that I have worked with over the years that actually does what it claims to do and backs it up. It is a product called "Resist-All." From my experience this is the **only** product that will truly protect your paint and seal your fabric. I have seen it remove hard water stains from cars that are a few years old. I also had a customer once who left her windows open a crack during a rainstorm. Since she had Resist-All applied, the water that got into her car pooled onto her seats rather than seeping into them. She was able to wipe it up with a towel. This was when I started to believe in this product. They also warranty your seats against stains and punctures. No other product I have worked with has backed up their product like Resist-All does. If you feel you need this product, then make sure it is "Resist-All." If it is any other, then I do not recommend it.

The other types of fabric protection tend to be a useless product since your seats are usually already protected to the point where no other substance will make it any better. If you have leather seats then liquids can be cleaned up better than cloth seats because there is little to no absorption. This fabric protection product sells for anywhere from $300 to $500 or more, but the cost on this product is anywhere from $35 to $100. It is a pure profit maker for the dealer with very little value behind it. Dealers can be ruthless. I have even seen dealers sell the rust proofing protection on a Corvette. The problem is that Corvettes are made with fiberglass and therefore do not rust. They know this but recommend it to the customer anyway with the hope that they can make some profit from an unsuspecting customer.

LO-JACK

A Lo-Jack theft recovery system is another product offered by the Business Manager in many dealers. It is a little device that is hidden in your car in a place where only the installer knows. It is designed to help law enforcement recover your car once it is reported stolen by using this "tracking" device. It is activated once you report your car stolen so the police can track it using a tracking device in their police cruiser. Remember, it is a "theft recovery" device which means it comes into play once the car is reported stolen. It does nothing to deter the theft of your car. It is a reliable device as it has a recovery rate of over 90%. The problem is that coverage does not extend to all areas in the U.S. It is mainly in the most populated areas of the country. They are expanding into Europe and they also have devices for motorcycles.

The other problem you have with Lo-Jacks is it does not get activated until you report your car stolen. So if you get into work at 9am and your car is stolen at 10am, but you get out of work, notice it stolen, and report it at 5pm, then the thieves have a 7 hour head start. Who knows how far away they could be, or maybe even have your car stripped by then? There is an early warning system that they offer to alert you if your car is moved which would help solve this which costs a few hundred dollars more. This is a pretty expensive system as it generally runs about $700 for a basic system and about $1000 for the basic system with the early warning system.

These products are generally marked up about $300 or more so there is room for negotiation here as well. This could be of value to you if you get a discount on your insurance which helps offset the cost. Some states have mandatory discounts on your comprehensive coverage of your car insurance, not the full policy. You need to take your discount per year and multiply it by the number of years that you plan on owning the car. **If that number is greater than your negotiated price, it may be worth the investment.** Otherwise, check with your insurance company to see if you get a discount with the installation of a Lo-Jack. Here is some information on coverage area for Lo-Jack as well as insurance discount information by state:

STATEWIDE COVERAGE (OVER 80% OF THE POPULATION)

- Arizona
- California
- Connecticut

- District of Columbia
- Maryland
- Massachusetts
- Michigan
- New Jersey
- Rhode Island

MAJOR METROPOLITAN AREAS, CITIES AND HIGH CRIME AREA COVERAGE

- Colorado
- Northern Delaware
- Florida
- Georgia
- North Carolina
- Northeast Illinois
- Southeast Louisiana
- Washington
- Southern Nevada
- Southeast New Hampshire
- Southeast New York
- Southeast Pennsylvania
- Central Texas
- Virginia

INSURANCE DISCOUNTS:

Arizona: Up to 25%

California: Up to 33%

Colorado: Up to 25%

Connecticut: Up to 25%

Delaware: Up to 25%

District of Columbia: Up to 25%

Florida*: Up to 25%

Georgia*: Up to 25%

Illinois: Up to 25%

Louisiana: Up to 25%

Massachusetts*: Up to 35%

Maryland: Up to 25%

Michigan: Up to 25%

New Jersey*: Up to 25%

Nevada: Up to 25%

New Hampshire: Up to 25%

New York*: Up to 25%

Pennsylvania: Up to 25%

Rhode Island*: Up to 35%

Texas*: Up to 30%

Virginia: Up to 25%

*State mandates insurance discount

Source: Lojack.com

PREPAID SERVICE PLANS

Prepaid service plans are another product that dealers sell. These are plans that allow you to pay for your regularly scheduled maintenance upfront so when you come in for service you just give them a coupon and never have to pay any money down the road. This sounds convenient, but if you do the math with what the dealer charges, because his profit of at least a couple of hundred dollars is figured in, it really does not save you any money. Plus, there can be other issues such as it may only allow you 4 quarts of oil for an oil change when your car actually takes 5 quarts or it may take a different type of oil. If that is the case they are going to charge you more for that extra quart or different type of oil which now throws the savings out the window. **Also, know this: The dealer counts on the customer not showing up for all of the scheduled maintenance intervals. Any unused service intervals are now profit for the dealer.** This is a very common expectation for the dealer as this really is where the profit is made. It is just like getting a gift certificate and never using it. Stores plan on that and use the unused gift certificates as profit, with very special accounting practices that must be followed. These prepaid service plans really are not worth what they cost you.

What the dealers like most is that prepaid service plans keep you coming back for service visits resulting in profit for the dealer. Every time they visit they will offer more services that are not included in the package that you would have to pay for. Plus a customer is more likely to buy from the dealer where they do their service than any other dealer. The customer has built up loyalty over time and the dealer knows this. The service writers and manager are aware of this too. When an older car comes in or a large repair bill comes across their desk, they try to recommend you to talk to a salesman about buying a new car. This is very common in service departments when you are close to 100,000 miles. A car loses a lot of value when it hits 100,000 miles so they try to get you to talk to a salesman about buying a new one. Many dealers will give that service writer a "birddog" for referring the customer. A "birddog" is an amount of money such as $50 or $100 that he gets for the referral. This is an incentive for the service writer to do this plus it is another source of new car sales for the dealer.

ALARMS AND REMOTE STARTERS

Aftermarket alarms or remote car starters are offered by most car dealers. For the most part they are installed by an outside company but some dealers are able to install them themselves. An alarm may get you an insurance break with your insurance company but they really do not do much besides that. A professional car thief will most likely take your car no matter what theft deterrent device you have on it. No car is completely safe. Use your personal experience to determine if you need a car alarm. For example, the last time you went to the mall did you hear a car alarm going off? Pretty much everyone has. Did you turn your head and look at the car whose alarm was going off? Did you care? Exactly! Most people don't. A car alarm used to mean something when not many cars had them. Now you hear them going off in the middle of the night and no one even calls the police or looks out the window.

An alarm is not that effective unless it has a means of not only keeping your car from being stolen but getting people to pay attention as well. No car alarm is 100% guaranteed to make sure you car will not get stolen, it is another profit maker for the dealer. Not to mention the factory usually has a passive alarm system already installed that would do almost the same thing with no additional cost. A coded ignition key is usually the best way of someone not being able to steal your car. That way a key made without an encoded chip will not start the car, and neither will breaking the steering column. But like I said, if a professional car thief wants your car, he will likely get it no matter what alarm is on it.

A remote car starter is another dealer aftermarket item. This is strictly a convenience item. It allows you to start your car from inside your house or office by remote control so it can either warm up or cool down before you get into it. Most remote starters are from outside companies. A lot of them entail bypassing the security system in order to get them to work because many cars are designed to only be started with a key that has an embedded encoded security chip. They can not be started without that encoded key. The remote starter has to find a way to get around that system so the car starts without the key. This can get tricky and some wiring mix ups can be a real problem down the line with the rest of your car.

Also, many manufacturers will not sanction remote starters that are not factory original or installed. So a remote starter could in some cases void your factory warranty. Check with the manufacturer to see if that is the case with your model. Do not ask the installer from the store who installs it. **They will only tell you what you want to hear.** They want to make profit from the sale too. Manufacturers are now realizing that their customers are demanding this option so you are going to see remote starters becoming factory installed items in the future. This way they are covered by the factory warranty while keeping their customers happy. This price may vary by the level of other functions that the starter has. Remember, the price is negotiable. Mark up on these can average around a couple of hundred dollars.

BANK FEES

If you are using a bank or credit union to finance (i.e. Bank of America, JP Morgan Chase, Citizens Bank, Wachovia Bank) there may be an additional bank fee. This is usually called a "VSI fee." That stands for **V**endors **S**ingle **I**nterest insurance. VSI is basically a little insurance policy that the bank takes out on each customer in order to protect them if they have to repossess the car and it has disappeared and the bank can not find their property. This is a fee that is from the bank and not a fee from the dealer. This fee is not one that can normally be foreseen prior to the sale. It also varies from bank to bank. I've seen it as little as $35 and as high as $95. This goes up over time as losses increase over the years. This fee is not under the control of the dealer and they can not mark it up. This is just a pass on fee from the bank. Finance companies do not have VSI fees. There is an easy way to determine the difference between a bank and finance company. Banks have branches where you can walk in and do business while finance companies do not. Finance companies are generally manufacturer finance companies such as GMAC, American Honda Finance Corp., Toyota Motor Credit and VW Credit as well as some sub-prime finance companies like Americredit, HSBC Household Auto Finance and Capital One Auto Finance.

THE "SPOT DELIVERY"

If a dealer ends up doing a "spot delivery" with you, which means that you purchased the vehicle and took delivery of it within a short period of time on the same day, then there are certain things that you need to be aware of. First of all, I do not recommend letting the dealer make the process move that fast. The reason that they do this is that they want to keep your excitement flowing. Getting a new car is exciting for most people. The car is shiny and has that new car smell. You can't wait to drive it away and show your friends and family. The dealer knows this and tries to play on these emotions.

The problem is that your excitement actually works against you. Many customers will fall in love with a car and do whatever it takes to get **that car.** That is why the test drive is so important to the salesperson. He knows if you fall in love with the car, then you are putty in his hands. You are more likely to pay more than you can afford or buy more products than you need because you just want that car so badly. This is one of the reasons why a salesman will start you off in a base model and then move you to a mid level model and then the loaded model. This way you can see the difference and wind up craving the nicer model which gives the salesman more profit. However, this is where some of the real shenanigans start. You love the loaded model, but when you go into the business office and the Business Manager gives you the payment and you can not afford it, you get really disappointed

So now the Business Manager makes your "dream come true" by lowering the payment to a somewhat affordable level. It is still more than you can afford but you love the car and are willing to pay more for it. **You thought he lowered the price, but he really just lengthened the term of your loan to 72 months.** Then the Business Manager recommends you protect your car with a warranty and a LoJack or alarm. He tells you that you will save money on insurance and will not have to pay anything if the car breaks down. It sounds great since your car is the latest and greatest and should be taken care of and protected. But again the payment is too much. So the Business Manager again drops the payment. "Wow! What a deal!" you are thinking to yourself. Not really. **He just lengthened your loan to 84 months.**

Your payment is still more than you can afford and you still haven't realized that **this new car will raise your insurance,** and **you still need to pay sales tax.** You quickly sign the paperwork because the Business Manager says he has people waiting and that your car should be cleaned and ready to drive away in a few minutes. You are bursting with excitement so you sign everything without even looking at it. "I've got a new car!" you're thinking. You drive away with your new car thinking your dreams have come true and you want to show the world your car.

Meanwhile, the dealership is smiling because you were a dream customer who they probably made a $4000 - $5000 profit on a car that generally may not earn that much. Plus, because they spot delivered the car they guaranteed that you won't buy anywhere else. **But in reality you just made the worst investment of your life.** This happened because you let your excitement take over and caused you to lose your sense of reason.

When the excitement wears off and you look at your paperwork, get your new insurance bill and pay your sales tax you may get queasy when you realize what you did. At that point it is too late. You have made your purchase and now are stuck with it. You are even stuck with it for longer than you want because you financed so long that you always will owe a lot more than it is worth which makes it impossible to roll it into another car loan when you trade it in. Therefore, you are stuck with a car that no longer makes you excited and meanwhile the dealer is very happy to do your warranty work. **Do not ever let the dealer know that you are excited about a car.** They will use it against you just like in this instance. Slow the process down. Stay in control. The car will still be the same if you pick it up the next day rather than today. Your ability to reason will be back and you will make smarter decisions. This is a perfect time to use your poker face. What the salesman does not know will not hurt him. And before you dismiss this story as extreme or rare… let me assure you, this happens hundreds, if not thousands of times a day, every day, throughout the U.S.

What a dealer may sometimes have you sign is a "spot delivery" form. This is a form that states that right now you are not approved by a bank for financing but they are drawing up a finance contract anyway with an estimate of what your rate will be and have you sign it so you can drive it away. It basically says that when you get financed you may have to come back and sign a new contract with the correct figures on it. If you are not financed then you have to bring the car back. Dealers do this to take the shopper "off the road" and protect them from the customer buying elsewhere. This happens mainly when a customer had less than perfect credit and it may take some time to get them financed but this is not limited to that type of customer.

What usually happens is that they call the customer back in to sign the new contract and the rate and payment has gone up a large amount. The customer is so excited after driving that new car around all weekend and showing their friends and family, they do not want to go back and tell them that they had to give it back so they sign the paperwork anyway. This also worked in the dealer's favor because he played the customer on his ego and excitement. You have already taken "mental ownership" of the car so in your mind this car is yours and nobody will take it away from you. **This is a common ploy that works almost every time.** It is more successful with customers that have less than perfect credit because they know or think that their finance options are limited due to their credit scores. If they want you to sign one of these forms or waivers, then stop the process and tell them to contact you when they know that you are financed, including the rate and terms. This way you will know what you are getting and not an "idea" of what you are getting.

chapter four

HOW MUCH IS YOUR CAR WORTH?

TRADE-INS

When you first started this whole process, I told you not to let the salesperson know if you had a trade-in. Now I am going to explain why.

If you are trading in a car then you need to do and be aware of certain things. First of all, like I said before, do not tell your salesman that you are trading in a car. Park your trade across the street or in the back of the building or even in the service area where their customers park as long as it is out of view. You may even want to go to the dealership with a friend in your friend's car. Second, **make sure your research is done before you attempt to do this.** You need to get an idea of what your car is worth. Start with the most popular car guides which would be NADA (National Automobile Dealers Association) at www.nada.com, Kelly Blue Book at www.kbb.com, Edmunds TMV (True Market Value) at www.edmunds.com or Galves at www.galves.com. These books are the most popular ones used by car dealers to determine the value of your car.

Keep in mind that these books are merely guides. Just because the book says your car is a certain value, it does not necessarily mean that you will get that for a trade-in. Many dealers use local auction reports to get a value since they are more of a true test of what cars are selling for at the time. These reports show what other dealers are paying for similar cars at a wholesale level, because you will get wholesale value when you trade in your car. You usually will not get more than that. The reason is that the dealer needs to buy the car at a price where they can turn around, bring it up to standard in the service department and then make a profit on it when it is sold on the lot.

Even if they chose not to sell it on their lot, they still need to sell it to a wholesale dealer that will in turn sell it on his lot or to another dealer who can sell those types of cars. If they don't take that route, then the last resort is the auction block. That is why the auction reports are important to a dealer. When you look the value of your car up in the guides, you need to use trade-in value, not retail value. Retail value is a value you may be able to get if you sold it privately. Trade-in value is the value you car may be worth if you chose to trade it in.

The problem with the guides is that some don't take into effect the condition of the vehicle. Most guides show a value for an average condition vehicle. Most cars that are traded in are not in average condition. The dealer either adds or deducts from the value based upon the condition of the vehicle, and what you may consider average condition may not be average condition to the dealer. The dealer also wants to own the car for as cheap as possible so they can get more profit when they sell it. There a few things that dealers will do to make sure this will happen.

The first thing they do is when they look at your car they will do what is called "devaluing" the car. This is what the salesman or manager will do when they look at your car for the first time. What that entails is walking around your car in a place where you can see them. Then while he walks around your car he will touch or run his finger over every tiny flaw on your car. He may open your hood or check the depth of your tire tread. The more he touches, the better for him because what this is doing is making you think that your car is in worse condition then you think it really is. Therefore, they have "devalued" the car and made your expectations lower than what you originally thought.

The guides (NADA, Kelly Blue Book, Galves, etc.) will show you a retail value, a trade value and some will show you a loan value. Retail value is an estimate of what you could sell the car for on a retail level on a private sale or what a dealer may sell it for. Trade value is an average value of what you may be able to trade the vehicle in for. These numbers are not set in stone and the guides do not back them up in the sense that they would buy your car for the value that they say it is. Your car is worth what someone is willing to pay for it. The one thing I can almost guarantee you is that you will get more for your car if you sell it privately yourself then if you trade it in. So don't go to a dealer thinking that you will get retail value for your car. You will be disappointed. Just remember that these guides are just that, a guide. They are not the final and true value for all cars. It is merely a point to start for the dealer and the consumer.

Some of these online guides such as Kelly Blue Book may allow you to consider the quality of the vehicle in the value. The problem here is that everyone puts in "excellent" as the condition. No used car is in excellent condition unless it just rolled out of the factory with no scratches, dings or dents. Every car has wear and tear and that needs to be taken into consideration. So an average to below average rating usually is more of a true grading of what your car is.

If you are trading a car you should clean it up both inside and out. Now in some cases you might not want to clean it up. If it has a lot of dents or scratches, you may want to leave your car dirty so those may not be as obvious. Don't go through all the trouble of having everything fixed on it unless your car is unsafe. The dealer will pick out everything that is wrong with it anyway. They look at hundreds of trade-ins a month so they know what to look for and how to pick apart a car.

The best way to counteract all of this is to know everything about your own car. Be honest about it but don't give up too much information. When was your last oil change? Did you change the timing belt at 90 – 100,000 miles? Has it been in any accidents? Some dealers will give you a questionnaire about your car and have you sign it in case you give them any false information about your car. They use everything you tell them or sign against you if they feel you are being untruthful and they will use it to put down your car and make you think your car is worth less than it really is. Whatever you do don't sign anything like this. **You are not required to sign it nor should you.**

Now if you are trading your car in, you need to wait until the salesman gives you his best price on the car you are buying. Once that happens, you can say to the salesman, "What if I trade my car in? How much would you give me for it?" This way it sounds like you are debating whether you are going to trade your car in or not. If they end up liking your car, then they may give you a little more for it to entice you to trade it in. The good thing is that doing it this way will give you the true value of what your car is worth. That way they don't fiddle with the numbers when in comes to trade difference.

Make sure they show you what they are giving you for a price for the car you are buying and then separately give you what they are giving you for your car. Don't let them give you a "trade difference." What a trade difference is them giving you a number like "$15,000 + trade." This means that they could be selling you the new car for $25,000 and giving you $10,000 for your trade. Therefore, there is a $15,000 difference. This really doesn't tell you much and is intended to make the numbers look better without actually telling you the real numbers. That way it also makes you harder to shop the numbers because you really don't know what the numbers are.

What you are really looking for by handling the trade this way is the "ACV" or **A**ctual **C**ash **V**alue of your trade. This is the real value that the dealer has valued the car at. The ACV is not always the number that you will get. This is how the dealer makes that value mysterious. First of all, the salesman is trained to find your "hot button." Your hot button is the part of the deal that you are fixated on and will probably make the difference of whether you buy the car or not. It could be monthly payment, price of the car itself, value of the trade or maybe even options on the car or color. A lot of customers will want enough value from their trade in order to pay off the loan on it. Many customers make the mistake of thinking that the value of your car is what you owe on it. That is the farthest from the truth. A dealer may play on this by giving you what you owe on your vehicle but he is charging you MSRP or higher for the new car in order to offset the high amount you owe on the car.

For example, this is what it may look like on a car with a $25,000 MSRP with a car being traded in with an Actual Cash Value (ACV) of $10,000 and the salesman has figured that your "hot button" is your trade in value:

Sale Price: $27,000

Trade-in value: $12,000

Trade difference: $15,000

Here, the dealer made this deal look great because you got $12,000 for your trade in. You may have expected to get $11,000 for it so you are happy. You think that you pulled one over on the dealer so you sign the Purchase and Sale Agreement before you think they realize what they did. But what you didn't realize is that you paid $2000 over sticker price for your new car. Even though they gave you $2000 more than the value they placed on it, they made it up by raising the sale price by $2000. Therefore, the dealer still sold the car at full sticker price. You thought you got a good deal but the dealer really got the good deal here.

Here is another example with the same situation but with the salesman figuring your hot button is the price of the car you are buying:

Sale Price: $23,000 (Remember MSRP is $25,000)

Trade-in value: <u>$8,000</u>

Trade difference: $15,000

In this situation, you feel you got a good deal because you got a $2000 discount on the car. But in reality, the dealer "held back" $2000 on the value of your trade to make up for the discount. This still is a sale at full sticker price. The bottom line is the same on both examples. It is just moving the numbers around in order to satisfy the needs of the customer. This is the most common method used by dealers. It also is the most likely situation you will be in. This is how a dealer can show you an invoice and say "We are selling this car to you for less than we own it for!" In reality they are holding back on the value of your trade in order to make up the discount. **This is the most common way that a dealer can make money on a deal when a trade is involved. It gives them another way to "work the numbers" and make it look enticing to you.** You're car may be worth $10,000 but they are really giving you $8000. That is now a $2000 profit to the dealer just on the trade alone. They can sell the car for $500 below invoice and still make a $1500 profit.

Here is another example with the same situation but with the salesman figuring your hot button is the payment limit of $300:

Sale Price: $25,000

Trade-in value: $9,000

Monthly payment: $275

In this situation, you feel you got a good deal because your payment came out to $275 which is $25 less than you wanted to pay. But in reality, they charged you full sticker price, held back $1000 on the trade in and then stretched your finance term out from 60 months to 72 months or even 84 months. The dealer now charged the customer sticker price and increased their finance income by stretching the finance term out to 72 months. Since you are comfortable with a $300 payment you still have $25 per month for the Business Manager to sell you more products to add to the profit. They may even tell you that your payment is $300 so the Business Manager has an easier time selling products to you because your payment will not go up much, making the products look more enticing. This is a very lucrative deal for the dealer.

I'm going to show you my method of dealing with this so the dealer can't do anything like this to you. After you get your best price on the car you are buying, tell the dealer you have a trade-in and see what they give you for a value. If they know you are shopping, because you already told them, then they should give you the full value of your trade. If they try to hold back on you then they risk the chance of losing the deal. So chances are pretty slim that they would hold back on you. Make sure they give you the trade value separate from the sale price of the vehicle. Don't let them give you a confusing bunch of numbers that disguises the real numbers.

VALUE OF YOUR TRADE-IN

When you are going to trade in your car there are several factors you should know that affects the value of your trade. The first and most obvious is the condition of the vehicle. The second factor is the mileage. Is the mileage on the car above average? Average mileage is considered to be about 15,000 miles a year. If your trade-in is way above average, then this can affect the value of your trade because a dealer may not be able to or want to sell it on their lot as a used vehicle. If it is under the average, then it can be worth more as it is a good car to sell on the lot. A dealer will keep good cars on the lot and will sell ones they can't keep to wholesalers. A car that a dealer wants for sale on their lot is more likely to get more value for their trade-in from a dealer than one that they don't want.

You also need to know what you owe on your car. Call your bank and get a payoff from them. This way you know if you are in a "negative equity" situation. This is when you owe more than the car is worth. Instead of having equity, you have negative equity. It is also referred to as being "upside down." The payoff on the car is not the fault of the dealer, but the value they give you for your car is. This negative equity will need to be added to the financing unless you have the money to pay it down or pay it off. If it is too much more than the value of your trade, then you may be in a position where you may not be able to finance it in to your loan. The banks only give you a certain percentage over retail price of the car you are buying. If you are over that you may be out of luck. If your credit is less than perfect that percentage goes even lower.

Another factor is trading your brand of vehicle into a dealer that is the same brand as yours. For example, trading a Honda into a Honda dealer. That dealer may be willing to pay more for your trade because they need that type of car for their used car inventory. They know more about the car that you are trading in than someone familiar with another brand. This could even work, for example, if you trade in a Honda for a Nissan but that dealership is a dual make store where they sell Hondas too. They may give you more for your Honda than a store that is just a Nissan store. So trading in your car at a dealer that is the same brand as yours may give you a little bit more value for your car than at others.

Another factor to look at is options on your trade that are region specific. What I mean by that is certain options that a car may have can affect the value of your trade. For example, if you try to trade in a 2WD truck or SUV in the North, it will be worth much less than what you would get down South. The demand for a 2WD truck in the North is very low and rare. They do sell, but not often enough for dealer to want to have it sitting on their lot for several months until that one unique buyer comes along. The same school of thought goes for trading in a 4WD truck down South. The 4WD gives you no more value down South than a 2WD truck. A trade-in without air conditioning will be almost useless in the South but it may not be a huge difference up North. Some areas in the far North may even have a need for engine block heaters which could add value. So be aware that certain options that have demand in certain regions of the country may have no demand in another part of the country.

Trade-ins can also be affected by seasonal demand as well. For example, if you try to trade your convertible or sports car in during the Fall or Winter, you will not get as much for them since demand for those vehicles is not very strong then. Those should be traded in during the Spring or early Summer months. The same is true for SUV's or trucks. If you try to trade them in during the Spring or Summer, then you won't get as much for them either. You should trade these in during the Fall and early Winter months. Dealers will change their values for a trade based upon seasonal demand. Two exact same cars traded in at different times of the year can have vastly different trade-in values.

Now that you have the numbers for your trade-in vehicle, you need to look and compare them the same way you did with your prices on purchasing your new car. Take all of your quotes from all of the dealers and look at the bottom lines. Take the sale price of the car and subtract what they are going to give you for your trade. This should give you your bottom line figure. The bottom line figure is how you will rank your quotes. You should now go through the same process we did before. Take the #1 quote and call the #2 quote to see if they can beat it. Go through all the quotes and give them all the opportunity to give you a better price. Someone may be crazy enough to blow the competition out of the water. This may be done by your local dealer as he wants your business more than anybody. The rest just follows the same process as explained earlier. The only thing that is not under the control of the dealer is what you owe on your car. So even though you have a trade difference, you still need to add in what you owe on your car and that is what you would be looking to finance. But what you owe should never be figured into your deal with the dealer. They will just make it more confusing for you. Whoever you finance with will be paying the vehicle off so you can deal with it when you get to that point.

Make sure at delivery that if you a paying off your trade-in that you sign and take a copy of the payoff paperwork. It is usually called an "Authorization for Payoff." This allows the dealer to pay off your car and have the title sent to them. Signing this form is the same as signing the back of title over to the dealer. The form looks different and may vary in name from state to state. You should keep a copy in case the dealer does not pay off the car. This will be your proof in case they don't pay it off. It should also be stated on the Purchase and Sale agreement.

THE 100,000 MILE PROBLEM

If you plan on trading your car in and it has more than 100,000 miles on it, then you need to be aware of how it affects the value of your car. You can still use the car guides to get an idea of an approximate value of what your car is worth but your car is worth what someone is willing to pay for it. The problem is that these books are misleading to consumers because they are just merely a guide as to what your trade is worth. None of these guides will actually pay you what your car is listed for in the guide. If your car has over 100,000 miles on it then you can almost throw the guides out the window on most cars. Cars that have over 100,000 miles can generally only be sold to wholesalers and can not be financed at a traditional dealership.

You can also check the local papers to see what cars like yours are going for. It is no secret to anyone that you will get more for your car selling it privately then trading it in. The reason for this is when a dealer takes a car in trade he is figuring that he needs to make a profit off it when he sells it as well as spending money to bring the car up to a condition where he can sell it off the lot. The dealer may need to put new tires on, change the timing belt or replace a windshield to name a few. Generally, trade-ins are not sold off the lot. They are sold to wholesalers or go to auctions to be sold. So in reality, your car is worth what the market will bear, and the used car market does fluctuate regularly. You can use your online sources to get an idea of what your car is worth, but the best way is to shop your trade around to dealers.

SELLING YOUR CAR PRIVATELY

If you have the ability to sell your car privately, no matter how many miles are on it or in what condition it is in, then do so. You will always get more selling it privately then you will if you trade it in. You can sell your car close to retail value when you sell it privately vs. getting trade-in or wholesale value when you trade it in. The problem usually lies with the consumer not having the time or ability to sell it privately. The best way to sell it privately would be to label your car with a fair price and park it in a highly visible spot. A good place is next to a busy road. This is tough for a lot of people because they don't have the ability to part with their car for a period of time because it is their primary or only means of transportation. You may also not have a lot of time to field phone inquires or make appointments to show people your car. You will also have to keep your car spotless if you want to show your car on a regular basis. You need to make sure there is no junk in it such as empty coffee cups, candy wrappers or anything that makes the car smell like anything but fresh. You also may need to spend some money in order to fix certain things in order to bring it up to a condition so you can show it. All of this may be more than some people want to go through, so they choose to trade in their car.

There are some other downfalls to selling your car yourself. First, you may lose out on a tax incentive. If you pay sales tax on your car, you probably will not be able to credit the value of a car you sell yourself against the sales tax of your new car.

For example:

Buying new car for $25,000

Sales Tax paid at 5% with no trade in: **$1250**

Buying new car for $25,000

Trade in valued at $10,000

Sales Tax paid at 5% on difference: **$750**

So you can see in this example that you could hypothetically lose out on a $500 tax savings. This loss could be greater as the value if your trade-in goes up or your tax rate goes up. So you need to make sure that you can get an amount more for your car by selling it privately than trading it in that will offset the tax loss. In this case you would need to get at least $500 more for your trade by selling it rather than trade it in order to benefit from a private sale.

DONATING YOUR CAR

You also may get a better tax break if you donate your car rather than trade it in. Some cars are in a condition where the dealer really does not want it. The car may be ready for the junkyard or they may not have a wholesaler that won't take a car in that condition. This is especially true if the car is not drivable. Every part of the country has a charity or organization that will come to your house and tow your car away and bring it to an auction to sell it. You will benefit by having the ability to use the value of that car as a tax deductible donation on your income tax statement. New IRS tax laws allow you to only take the actual sale price of the vehicle at auction rather than full book value like you used to. This value is usually much lower than book value because of auction fees and vehicle condition. Check with your accountant if you wish to do this in order to make sure you can take advantage of this tax break. Some dealers have contacts at local charities that will provide this service. This helps the dealers in the sense that they will take some of the cars that the dealer doesn't want, therefore not clogging up their inventory. It benefits the charities for obvious reasons. Some of them will even let you choose what charity you want the proceeds to go to. The dealer does not make any money from this. They only supply a means to an end.

ONLINE AUCTIONS OR ADS

Other ways to sell your car are by using online auctions or classified ads. Some of the better services out there are eBay Motors, Vehix, AutoTrader, Cars.com and Yahoo. There are several different services out there, you just need to find the one that has the most exposure and traffic. The only downfalls with auctions are that they are generally national auctions. Most people won't travel across the country to purchase a vehicle unless it is a very unique car with very high demand. That is usually reserved to high end exotic cars. I found eBay Motors to be a great source for selling a car that is under $10,000. The others mentioned are still good but are more recommended for cars priced over $10,000.

You are more likely to sell your car locally than nationally. That is why local newspapers or want ads may be more successful. There are occasions that I have seen where people will travel half way across the country for a car that they may not be able to get in that area due to high demand. They may be willing to pay more than you could get in your area. This is more the exception then the norm. So don't hold out for it but it may happen when selling a car privately.

No matter how you advertise your car, you need to be as thorough as possible as well as putting up as many pictures as you can. People are more interested in cars that have more information for them to process and picture in their mind. You also need to respond to any inquiries, whether it is by phone or email, as quick as possible. The reason is that you are competing with thousands of other cars out there as well. So if you don't get back to them, someone else might and you may miss an opportunity to sell your car. Selling your car yourself can be time consuming and bothersome, but the payoff can be well worth it.

PRICING STRATEGY

If you are going to sell your car privately, you need to price it accordingly. Do not plan on getting what you owe on it if your loan payoff is above retail value. What you owe is not what the car is worth. You should price it around retail value because your potential buyers will be looking at the guides as well. They know what your car is worth too. You should use a number that isn't a "dealer" type number such as $9,995. Use $10,000 or $9500, but your price should still be below retail value to give the incentive to someone to buy from you rather than a dealer. This is more realistic and shows that you want to do business. Try to put the number at about $500 higher than you want for the car. This leaves room for negotiation. Don't put in your ad "Best Offer." That tells any potential buyers that you are desperate to sell your car and you will get offers that are thousands below book value because they think they are going to get an incredible deal.

chapter five

YOU TAKE THE GOOD, YOU TAKE THE BAD...

THE POWER OF THE SURVEY

Once the sale is completed at the dealership, you think that your relationship with the dealer is over. But there is still one more powerful tool that may help you in case there is a problem with the dealer. It's called the "factory survey." Most people think of this as a useless piece of paper that you may fill out if you hated your car buying experience. This can actually be used to your advantage if you use it right. If there is a problem after you have taken delivery of your car and signed the paperwork, you may think that you are up the creek without a paddle. Most times a dealer will try to make things right with you if you find a problem, with the idea that you will refer friends and family there if your experience is good.

If the dealer chooses to play hardball and not fix something that was broken or to fix paperwork that may have been incorrect, then you have the survey as ammunition. Every dealer wants a perfect survey. They are scored by that survey and they go through a lot to make sure you know that they need a perfect survey from you. They may even show you a copy of the survey that is highlighted where you should mark it so they get a perfect score. So they usually want to rectify any problem that you may have prior to that survey showing up at your house.

The reason for the survey being important is that the factory is tying it to other incentives that the dealer gets. Each factory is different but they rank each dealer according to average score. The lowest scored dealers may be punished by getting their allocation of new cars lowered or changed. They may lose out on advertising money or their ability to get port cars. Port cars are cars that are set aside by the factory for dealers that need cars and whose inventory is low. These are extra cars that the factory will give to dealers to help them out so they have extra inventory to sell and make additional profit. Their allocation is what the manufacturer assigns them for cars. They obviously want the cars that are selling, but they could end up with some cars that have few options or unpopular colors. Advertising money is important because you need to advertise to sell. There are also incentives given to dealers who reach certain levels of high survey scores. The incentive to some of these large dealers can amount to over $100,000 a year or more. That is a great deal of money to lose due to bad surveys. Anything that may cause a dealer to make less profit will cause them to do anything to avoid being in that situation. Hence, the power of the survey.

You may be thinking "But I'm only one survey." You may be one survey but you are not the only person who may be upset about their experience. For a smaller to medium size dealer this is more prevalent since the scores are averaged out over time. A smaller dealer has fewer surveys to average out the bad ones so they will always work harder to make things right if the survey is hung over their head. Larger dealers have more surveys to average out the bad ones so they may not be as accommodating, but if it gets to the point where you are unhappy and the survey is your only weapon, then you should contact the General Sales Manager or General Manager of the dealership. These people usually don't get calls from customers but when they do, they usually act swiftly since if a customer is upset enough to call them then they feel it is a serious issue that needs to dealt with swiftly no matter how minor it may appear.

You don't need to be threatening when you talk to anyone at a dealer, you could tell them the story of your problem and then slip in the phrase, "I have this survey sitting in front of me and I'm not sure how I plan on filling it out. This situation doesn't make me feel good about it." This gets you farther than "I'm going to give you a bad survey if you don't fix this!!!" This makes them think that even if they rectify the problem, they will still get a bad survey. So the dealer would be less likely to help you. Be diplomatic and calm. As the saying goes, "You can catch more bees with honey than you can with vinegar." So use the survey as a means of power over the dealer after the sale is completed in order to rectify a problem that is a legitimate issue. It has more power than you may think. Factories are holding the dealers more accountable for surveys now more than ever. The reason is that with such a competitive market, it sometimes can come down to a customer's experience at the dealer that can make the difference in the success of the manufacturer's business. So the manufacturers use surveys to make the dealers change their ways and treat their customers better.

Unfortunately there are dealers that will not change their ways and continue to treat customers badly. The dealer can usually tell when they will get a bad survey. So they try to beat the system when this happens. I've seen dealers put in a fake address when the car is reported sold so the survey goes to the wrong address. A lot of times the salesman may use his own address just so he can fill it out and guarantee a perfect survey. Some of the manufacturers are switching over to phone surveys as they feel this will fix the problem of the "wrong address" and is more likely to get the customer to answer the survey. Unfortunately, the dealer can just change one digit on the phone number and the same result will occur. Or like the last example, he can use the salesman's number to guarantee himself a perfect survey.

Not all dealers do this, but it is known to happen from time to time from some of the less reputable dealers. The problem with this is that if the dealer does not fix the address and name later, any correspondence from the factory may not get to you such as recall notices or it may even affect a warranty claim down the line.

FINANCE VS. LEASE

You may be debating on whether to finance or lease your vehicle. There are different schools of thought for both methods. First, you need to know what both methods are. Financing a car is the most traditional method used and is very simple. You purchase a car, put money down and borrow the rest of the money from a bank for a set period of time and make payments over that time until it is paid off. At the end of the loan you don't need to make any more payments and you own your car until it either dies, you sell it, total it or trade it in.

Leasing is a little different and is more complicated. In a lease, you actually pay for the depreciation of a car over a set period of time, usually 24 – 36 months. Basically, in a lease you have different terms that need to be defined. First, you have a gross capitalized cost (cap cost) which is your sale price. Second, you have your capitalized cash reduction (cap cost reduction) or down payment. Third, you have your residual value which is a percentage of the MSRP that the leasing company figures to be the value of the car at the end of the lease. Fourth is the money factor which is basically your interest or finance rate. A money factor is a percentage rate that the lease is figured upon. It may be number such as .00275. This can be translated into a percentage rate by taking that number and multiplying it by 2400. (.00275 x 2400 = 6.6%) Some of the domestic manufacturers will use a percentage rate when figuring the lease while the foreign manufacturers usually use a money factor. The interest or finance charge on a lease contract is usually referred to as the "rent charge."

Basically, in a lease you are paying for the use (or depreciation) of the car for a set period of time such as 36 months. The lease company, which is usually the factory bank (Ford Motor Credit, American Honda Finance, GMAC, etc.) since they generally have the best programs, sets the residual percentage. This is not negotiable. So if you are looking to lease a car with a $20,000 MSRP for 36 months and it has a residual value of 45%, then the bank figures the car will be worth $9000 in 3 years. So you are paying for only $11,000 of use rather than the full $20,000 of use. Therefore, your payment is less than if you financed the vehicle.

Now the payment can go lower if you get a lower sales price and get a lower money factor. This negotiation is no different than when you finance a car, the only problem is that with a lease, you almost always will have to go through the dealer as they will have the best program from the manufacturer. So you need to be more cautious and ask a lot of questions. What is my sale price? What is the money factor? What is the residual percentage? How much is my acquisition fee? Is this a closed end lease? How many miles a year is this lease? How many months is this lease?

When you are looking to lease you need to make sure you are getting a closed end lease. A closed end lease is a lease where the actual value of the car at the end of the lease is at the risk of the lease company, not the customer. These are the most common leases. Open ended leases are where the value of the vehicle at the end of the lease is the responsibility of the customer. These were popular many years ago. I an open-ended lease, the customer owed a large amount of money at the end of the lease. This was because the customer would have to pay the difference of the residual value and the sales price at the auction. Or, they made the mistake of not buying enough miles on the lease and they went over. This is why people who leased vehicles many years ago or heard stories of people who were in these situations believe that leasing is not a good thing.

You need to determine how many miles a year that you drive if you wish to lease a car. The easiest way is to take the mileage of the car you are driving now and divide it by the years you have been driving it. For example, if you have put 37,500 miles on your car and you have been driving it for 2 ½ years, then you would be driving 15,000 miles a year (37,500/2.5 = 15,000). You also should figure any lifestyle changes over the next few years that may affect your miles driven such as job changes, relatives moving closer or farther away and even the location of your significant other. All of these locations can move closer or farther away and can affect the miles that you drive. If you have an idea of these factors then you should try to figure how they may affect you mileage. If you are unsure then you should buy more miles than you need. If you buy extra miles at the beginning of the lease they are cheaper than if you are penalized at the end of the lease. If you go over on miles, the bank will charge you for them and they usually cost more on the back end then they do when you buy them up front.

The first mistake people make when leasing a car is that they negotiate the payment and mileage. When you lease a car, you still can use all the tools

I gave you to negotiate your best price. The mistake made is when customers don't negotiate the price so they end up paying more than if they purchased the car. Dealers love lease customers. First of all, they generally get more profit from the sale of the car because a payment is negotiated rather than a price. Second, they get a good used car back in 2 to 3 years that should be in good condition and have average miles. It's a perfect car for their used car inventory. Third, they get another potential customer to either sell or lease another car to in 2 to 3 years. If you financed your car then they may not see you for 4 to 5 years or even longer.

There are several reasons why people lease a car rather than financing it. First, since the payments are lower, you can afford a more expensive car without the large expense. Second, you need little to no money down when leasing a car. Third, this is the best way to get a new car every 2 – 3 years. Fourth, your maintenance expenses are lower because you generally don't go that far out of the factory warranty, if at all. Fifth, almost all leases include Gap Insurance in case there is a total loss of the vehicle and you owe more then the car is worth. Sixth, the value of the car at the end of the lease is not your risk or responsibility. If the market crashes and the value (residual value) of your car plummets, then the bank will take the hit, not you. On the other hand, if the value of your car is higher than the residual value at the end of the lease, you can buy the car and then sell it privately and make a profit.

Here is a comparison of lease payments vs. finance payments on a car valued at $23,000:

	Lease:	0% loan:	6% loan:
Price:	$23,000	$23,000	$23,000
Down Payment	$1000	$1000	$1000
Interest Rate:	6%	0%	6%

Residual:	$11,000	N/A	N/A
Months:	36	36	36
Payment:	**$388.06**	**$611.11**	**$669.28**

As you can see, the difference in payments is pretty large. This is just an example so the numbers can vary depending on the type of car you are looking to lease. Foreign cars tend to lease better than Domestic cars due to residual values. Foreign cars generally hold their value better than a domestic which makes leasing a good investment. Domestic cars can be leased; their products are just not as competitive.

Most leases will require a security deposit which will be equivalent to the monthly payment rounded up to the next $25. For example, if your payment is $332 a month, then your security deposit will be $350. This is a refundable deposit which the lease company should give back once the car is turned in at the end of the lease. A lot of leases have the option of waiving your security deposit by slightly raising your money factor. It may raise your payment by a couple of dollars but it is less money that you need to pay at signing. Some lease companies will waive your security deposit if you have leased with them before. If you can avoid not paying a security deposit, then do so. **Lease companies make a great deal of money from unclaimed security deposits each year.** Don't let them have more money of yours to hold onto than they need. They can make interest off of all the security deposits they hold, too.

Also, if you have any damage on your car that they find to be excessive, they will charge you for it. They usually do this by taking it out of your security deposit. If they already have your money, than it can put you in a bad position if you need to fight the charges. If they don't have your security deposit as a ransom, then you are in a better position to fight or negotiate a damage claim made against you. If there is not a claim made by the lease company then you need to make sure that you contact them in order to make sure they send the deposit back. That is why I recommend not paying a security deposit.

Keep in mind, when you lease, you are more or less "renting" the car. So your payments are paid ahead a month, just like they are when you rent an apartment. You pay in advance. If you finance, then you pay in "arrears" which means you pay after the fact, or starting the month after you purchase your car. On a lease, you will need to make your first payment at delivery. But on the other end, you make your final payment and then you still have the car for another month before you need to turn it in.

Most people object to leasing because of false assumptions or bad experiences. Some of these problems could have been avoided if the customer was more aware of what a lease is all about. A salesman probably misled the customer or wasn't as thorough as they should have been in explaining their options. What I've seen happen many times is a customer wants a particular car really bad. They can't afford the payment but they want the car no matter what. The salesman will flip the customer into a lease with an affordable payment. The customer is mesmerized by the perfect payment for their perfect car and agrees to it even though they drive 20,000 miles a year and the lease is a 12,000 mile a year lease. At the end of the lease they finally realize the mistake they made and therefore will never lease again. This is the most common story from customers who do not like to lease.

There also several benefits to leasing that people may or may not be aware of. A lot of customers think they can't lease because they drive too many miles. This is not always the case because you can buy extra miles on the lease. You are not limited to 12,000 or 15,000 miles a year. I have had customers lease a car with a mileage limit of 30,000 miles a year. It was cheaper for them to purchase the miles up front then to pay a penalty at the lease end. Miles are generally 5 to 10 cents cheaper per mile if you buy them up front rather than at the end. So if you do a 3 year lease at 30,000 miles a year, the extra miles could cost you $4500 more at the end of the lease than if you purchase them at the beginning of the lease (15,000 miles/year (additional mileage) x 3 years = 45,000 miles x $.10/mile = $4500). Also, when you purchase more miles upfront, when you turn your car in, you don't have to listen to a dealer say "Your car isn't worth much because of the high mileage." You just turn it in and the lease company has to worry about what it is worth. Not you.

Some customers say that they never end up owning the car when they lease it. This is true, but what people don't realize is that the average customer only keeps their car for about 4 years. The average loan is over 5 years. So in reality, if you trade your car in 4 years but take a 5 year loan, then you never own it anyway. But you have managed to pay $100 more per month for the same use of that car. With a lease, you could have paid less for the same use. If you purchased the car, when you go to trade it in and you may owe more than it is worth. Now you need to roll that outstanding balance into a new loan and your payments are even higher. In a lease this never happens because you don't have the chance of having "negative equity" because you don't own it. So it can actually work in your favor.

You also may be able to get certain accessories on your car that can be "residualized" which can save you money over financing. Certain accessories such as spoilers, air conditioning, stereo upgrades, and other items that may enhance the value of the car over a longer period than normal can be added into the residual percentage. When the residual percentage is higher, the amount of the lease is less because you are leasing the value of the difference between the sale price and the residual value. By adding in these accessories your payment goes up less than if you financed it.

Another benefit to leasing is the tax advantage. When you lease and you write off your vehicle as a business expense, you generally can write off the entire payment on a lease. The reason is that on a lease you are paying for depreciation which is tax deductible. You don't always have that ability on a finance payment. So you may have the ability to write the entire payment off as a business expense. You should always check with your accountant before you do this in order to make sure you are making the right decision and qualify for the write off. Many people lease with this tax break in mind.

You also may pay less in sales tax. Every state is different on how they collect taxes on a lease. Generally, you only pay tax on the portion of the car you are using. It is sometimes figured by taking the total of all of the payments plus the cap cost reduction (money down) and then you figure the sales tax on that amount. It is figured on the money down because that money lessens the amount leased so they need to make sure that is accounted for. Some states require you to figure the sales tax into the monthly payment while others want it all up front at time of registration.

Here is an example:

	Lease:	**Purchase:**
Price of the car:	$20,000	$20,000
Lease payment:	$300	N/A
Term:	36 months	60 months
Sales Tax (5%):	**$540**	**$1000**

So you can see in this scenario there is a $460 savings in sales tax from leasing over financing a car.

There are also some drawbacks to leasing a vehicle. First of all, it is very hard to get out of a lease once you have entered it. A lease is a commitment for a set period of time. During that time you are required to make payments on that car. If you want to get out of the lease early, then you usually have to pay all of your remaining payments which can add up to a great deal of money. For example, if you are 12 months into a 36 month lease with a $300 monthly payment and want to get out of it, then you need to pay $7200 ($300 x 24 months = $7200). Sometimes if you are close to the end of the lease you may be able to trade the car in. This can happen if the actual cash value (ACV) the dealer places on it is greater than the balance of the payments plus the residual value. This would be the same amount if you want to purchase the car at the end of the lease. In this case the dealer would be buying it from the lease company.

You also gain no benefit in paying it off early or making extra payments. The total amount of your payments remains the same throughout the life of the lease. You can put extra in your payment, but it will not give you any savings like it would on a financed car. By financing you can pay extra and the car will be paid off earlier and you will pay less in interest. This is not the case with a lease. If you pay everything that is due all at once it will be the same if you pay it one payment at a time.

There are some companies out there that will help you get out of a lease that you are not happy with. There are two popular sites called www.swapalease. com and www.leasetrader.com. Both of these companies will help you get out of a lease by trying to find a "qualified buyer" to take over your lease for the remainder of the term. They both charge a fee for the service which can be in excess of a few hundred dollars, but it could be worth it if you want to get out of your lease. Laws on this vary from state to state and from lease company to lease company. I recommend you read your lease contract and consult the experts at these companies before committing a good portion of money to the process. These companies are both growing as the popularity of this is increasing.

At the end of the lease you may have to pay a "disposition fee." This is a fee that the lease companies will charge you when you turn in your lease. It is not a dealer fee. They usually offer to waive it if you either purchase your leased car or if you lease another car through them. This is supposed to offset the cost of transporting the car to auction amongst other costs. Some lease companies do not charge any disposition fees. You need to check with your dealer to see if there is a disposition fee on your lease. This fee even exists even of the dealer buys the car after the car is tuned in from the customer. Therefore there are no auction or transportation costs.

Putting money down on a lease gains you nothing other than a lower payment. Like I said before, the amount that you pay out on a lease will be the same no matter how much you put down. Since you are not gaining "equity" in your car in a lease, money down is not necessary or recommended. The only thing money down gives you is a lower payment because they just take the amount that you put down and divide it by the number of months and that is how much you lower your payments per month. For example, if you put $1000 down on a 36 month lease, then you just divide $1000 by 36, which means that you lower your payments by approximately $27.78. This may seem like a lot to some, but it gains you nothing in the long run. You can either keep that $1000 in your pocket, spend it on taxes or insurance or you can pay it and still have a payment due in a month. In other words, you should always lease a car with no money down. The only amount due at signing should be the first payment.

Each lease has an acquisition fee. These fees run from around $395 to as much as $895. All leases have these fees but they do range from lease company to lease company. The only thing to be careful of is that some banks allow the dealer to mark up the acquisition fee a few hundred dollars which they get to keep. The only way to counteract this is to shop around from dealer to dealer on your lease until the dealer gives up that markup in order to remain competitive.

Lease money factors work almost the same as finance rates. Money factors can be marked up just like finance rates. So the dealer can potentially make a profit off the lease itself as well as the car. Since you can't always lease through your local bank, you need to be competitive here too because the dealer is now your only source of leasing. You should pit the dealers against each other until they drop that markup to a point where they can earn your business. You will be surprised how fast they will drop it if it will hold you up from leasing a car. There are also special leases out there where the rates can not be marked up. These are special or sub-vented leases just like special or sub-vented financing on a car. These rates cannot be marked up by the dealer. Most dealers who advertise a lease will advertise a special lease because they can be very competitive. The programs do change from month to month depending on what cars the manufacturer needs to move for inventory. Those cars will generally have the best lease plans.

You may also be responsible for excessive damage to your car at the end of the lease. You car should be in average condition when you return it. Most lease companies will allow a certain amount of repairable damage up to a certain amount such as $1000 - $1500. Anything above and beyond that will be your responsibility to pay. Things such as body damage, bald tires, burn holes in seats, seat tears and broken windshields are some items that they can charge you for. So in a lease you need to keep your car in relatively good and clean condition or at least have it in that condition when you turn it in.

Leased cars generally require more insurance coverage than financed cars. First, their minimum coverage requirements are higher than if you finance. This is because the lease company is actually the owner of the car, so in the eyes of the laws of many states, they have vicarious liability -- That means that the owner of the car, the lease company, can be held liable for your negligence. For example, if you hit someone in your car and kill them, then not only you can be sued but the lease company can be sued as well. Usually when someone tries to sue, they go for the people with the deep pockets. Lease companies are usually the prime targets as they have more money than the average person. The added insurance coverage helps protect them in the event of something like that happening.

When you lease a car you are limited as to what you can do with a car as well. You can't change the color of the car, modify the suspension or exhaust or make any major structural changes to your car. This is because you need to give the car back at the end of the term. You also may be limited as to where you can drive it. Check the fine print on the back of the lease contract, but sometime you may need permission from the lease company if you want to drive the car out of the country or out of the contiguous 48 states. Not all lease companies rules are the same, so check with each one to see what their limitations are.

Some dealers will also try to put you into a "balloon note" and try to pass it off as a lease. A balloon note is similar to a lease in that you have use of the car for a set period of time, usually 36-48 months, and have a residual value and a rate that is slightly higher than a regular finance rate. You are allowed a certain amount of miles per year as well. The difference is that at the end of the term you owe a "balloon" payment of the remaining balance. This balance then either needs to be financed if you want to keep the car or you can turn it in and pay a fee and any other charges that are incurred such as mileage penalties or excessive damage.

If you choose to buy the car in a balloon note, then you have to finance the car and now are paying up to 8 years or more for the same car. Your total out of pocket expenses are now through the roof. The payments on a balloon note are usually a little higher than a lease. The reason why a dealer would push this or try to put you in one without knowing it is because of the way the car is registered.

On a balloon note the car is registered in your name, not the bank or lease company. The reason the factory likes this is because of vicarious liability. Like I just discussed, in some states, the owner of the car is responsible for the actions of the driver. In a lease that would be the lease company, but on a balloon note it is the customer. Therefore, the finance company that has the balloon note is not responsible for the negligent actions of the driver of the vehicle. They save themselves from any future civil actions and put the responsibility on the customer. You should always be specific when asking if they dealer is quoting a lease or a balloon note. Whether you choose a balloon note or a lease should be documented on the purchase and sale agreement. The dealer is required to note the amount due for the balloon payment at the end of the term of the note on your purchase and sale agreement and on the contract.

Financing is a better choice for a lot of people. Some people keep their car for longer periods of time. This is when financing a car and paying it off in time is a wise investment. They are generally content with having a mode of transportation and do not require the latest and greatest car out there. Some people have erratic driving habits where their mileage varies from time to time. Some people don't have enough credit to lease a car as their requirements for leasing are generally more stringent than financing. In some occasions leasing does not work out to be better because the programs that are out at the time just aren't competitive. A car may lease well this month but it may lease really bad next month.

Some customers like to buy their leased car at the end of the lease. Some people plan to do that from the beginning while others decide to do it at the end. I recommend against it. A lot of people that buy out their lease don't want their payments to go up. In order for this to happen you generally have to get a 5 year loan on the car. So after a 3 year lease you now have a 5 year car loan. That means that you are paying 8 years for your car. Now you have paid out more for your car then you would have if you financed it from the beginning, especially if the dealer talks you into buying an extended warranty or other products that I've discussed. In this case Gap Insurance is highly recommended because you will have negative equity in your car. In other words you owe more on your car than it is worth. So you may pay $2000 - $3000 in a rent charge for the lease and then pay another $4000 in interest to finance at the end of the lease. So you could pay up to $7000 in interest and rent charges, on the average, over the life of the car because you purchased it at the end. Therefore, you have lost all the money that you saved by leasing. You would have been better to lease another car, or even buy one, at a slightly higher payment and you would have spent less money and had a brand new car.

The biggest downfall in financing is that you are at the mercy of the market when it comes to figuring market value for your car. Your value of your car will not go up over time. 99.9% of the cars out there are depreciating assets where the value goes down over time. Your home is an appreciating asset, where the value of your home generally goes up over time. In a car loan, the loan gets paid down at a regular pace where the value of a car will depreciate at different rates over the life of the loan. Therefore, if you are in an accident and your car is a total loss, then there is a good chance that when you get your insurance settlement, the value of your car will not be enough to cover the balance of the loan. You will have negative equity. This is the biggest downfall to financing your vehicle. It is a risk that doesn't exist when you lease.

BUY NEW OR BUY USED?

One question that people ask all the time is whether they should buy a new car or a used car. It is an important question because people would like to know which one is a better investment. A lot of it depends on what your needs and wants are. Do you need the latest and greatest car? Are you specific on your car's options and color? How long to plan on keeping it? How well do you take care of your car? How picky are you about what type of car that you want?

Here are some points to consider with a used car. You may not get the latest style of car but you will spend less. You may not be able to get the exact color or options you want as well, so you need to be a little more patient and open to other colors or options. If you plan on keeping it for a while, you may want a car with lower miles and only a couple of years old. That way you have more life left in it to use. If you take care of your car very well then you may be able to get an older car for cheaper and it may still last you a long time. You need to be less picky as your choices may be limited to what is available in your area. You may also have to wait until the car you are looking for ends up on a lot somewhere.

The first good thing about buying a used car is that a used car has already suffered most of its depreciation. When a new car drives off the lot, it suffers anywhere from 10-30% of its depreciation immediately. The most depreciation of a car generally occurs in the first year, with the most being the day they drive off of the new car lot. The car is in the same condition, but it is worth much less; the original owner has absorbed most of the depreciation. Therefore, a used car is cheaper than a new car because it has already suffered most of its depreciation. Since you are buying this car used, the biggest chunk of the depreciation is gone and the car now depreciates at a steadier pace. This alone can make buying a used car a smart investment.

Another benefit to buying a used car is that you may spend less money on your car insurance since used cars generally have lower rates as they get older. You can also buy a nicer car with more options than you would if you purchased that "loaded" car brand new. So you can get more for less.

If you shop around you may be able to get a car that has just come off lease at a dealer. This means that you may be able to find a car that is a few years old with low or average miles that is good condition and has had only one owner. These cars are generally taken care of better since the owner knows that the car has to be in good condition when it comes off of lease. Maintenance is also done more regularly on a lease car for that same reason.

You may also be able to find a car that is still under factory warranty. Just because you are not the original owner doesn't mean that you can't take advantage of the factory warranty. If your car is still under factory warranty then you still have the ability to extend the factory warranty out to as far as 100,000 miles. If a used car is out of the factory warranty, then your warranty choices are somewhat limited. You almost always need to purchase the warranty at time of purchase if you are out of the factory warranty. The level of coverage gets less as the car gets older. You may be able to get bumper to bumper coverage while still under the factory warranty or just slightly out of it. But once the mileage and age goes up, your terms and coverage go down. You may have less coverage available, but still good coverage, with the terms being limited to shorter intervals such as 12 months/12,000 miles up to 48 months/48,000 miles. The older the car, the shorter the term that is available for coverage.

One of the downfalls of buying a used car is that your choices are more limited than with a new car. Buying a new car allows you to choose from many similar cars until you find the exact one you want. Used cars don't have that much variety and choices. You have to choose what is available. You may have to do more shopping in order to find the car that you want. Your concern really needs to be on watching out for cars that are involved in scams or major accidents. This is where your risk is the highest because you really don't know the history of the car. On a new car there is generally no history because you are the first owner. With a used car, you don't get a family tree nor do you usually get a maintenance history with the car. So it some cases in can be a crap shoot.

The best way to find a used car from your home is to use some of the online used car services on line. Some of the better ones are Vehix.com, Autotrader, Cars.com, Yahoo or eBay motors. The same services you use to sell your car could be the same one that you use to find the car you are looking for. The cars on these services usually have pretty good descriptions and pictures that you can use to see what it looks like and what is has for options. It also gives you an idea of what similar cars are selling for so you know what to expect when you find the car you want.

Whenever you buy a used car from a dealer, there will be a sticker on the window called a "Buyer's Guide" sticker. All used cars on a dealer's lot are required to have one. This sticker will show you some basic information about the car such as the year, make and model as well as the VIN. What the most important thing on that sticker is the warranty coverage. There will be 2 boxes on the sticker. One box, if checked, means that the car is being sold "as is." That means that there are no warranties on the car from the dealer. You are buying it as you see it. If it dies as you drive down the street, then the risk is completely on you, the buyer. The other box, when checked, means that there is warranty coverage on the car. It could say that there is still some factory warranty remaining until a certain mileage, or that the dealer is putting warranty coverage on the car. Then below this the warranty coverage will be broken out and disclosed. It may read something like, "3 month/3,000 mile powertrain coverage" and then it may list some of the parts of the car that are covered. Or it could say "balance of the 3 yr./36,000 mile factory warranty."

This sticker can give you some important information. From it you should be able to determine if a car is certified because the additional warranty will be broken out on the sticker. However, don't think that this sticker means that a car is in good condition. The quality of the car is not listed on the sticker. All the sticker is required to disclose is the warranty coverage. All dealers are required to have this sticker on all of their used cars that are on the lot. If they don't then they face some serious fines from the federal government.

HOW 9/11 CHANGED THE USED CAR MARKET

The used car market has changed dramatically since 9/11. That one tragic event changed the used car market for several years to come. What happened was the manufacturers came out with 0% financing right after 9/11. They did this in the hope of keeping the economy from crashing. What eventually happened was some of the best months for sales in the history of the car business. The down side to this was that most of the car buyers had a car to trade in. Therefore, the used car market was flooded with millions of cars. Using the rules of supply and demand, the supply was extremely high and demand was low which in turn drove the prices of used cars downward. Dealers were sitting on used car inventories that lost huge amounts in value. The auctions were also flooded with cars that were traded in which drove the auction prices down. So dealers were buying cars for less but in turn had to sell them for less because there were so many to choose from. That in turn caused the value of trade-ins at the dealer to be worth much less. They could not sell the cars for as much money anymore so they had to own the cars for less. Therefore, people were getting thousands less for their trade-in.

It took a long time for the market to clear out their inventory. But the damage was done. The market was affected to the point where used car values were brought down to point where the entire standard for used cars was changed.

This works well if you are buying a used car, but works against you if you are looking to trade in a car.

The same problem occurs when the manufacturers come out with their aggressive pricing campaigns. The biggest campaign was when "Employee Pricing" came out. This was when anyone could purchase a new car at the same price that the dealer employees could buy them at. It was a great deal because you got the absolute best price, set by the factory, without having to negotiate. With employee pricing, the dealers aren't even allowed to negotiate the price. The only problem is that with each positive move for the customer, comes a negative move for the customer. In this case, the employee price is approximately $1500 less than the average normal price paid by customers. This works well if you are just purchasing a car. It does not work well if you are trading in a car. Since the new cars now are an average of $1500 cheaper than they had been in years, now in order for used cars to remain competitive, they also had to be sold for about $1500 cheaper. Therefore, the dealers needed to own their inventory of used cars for cheaper. Whatever the incentive, the simple fact is the more cars that get brought into the used car market during these campaigns, the faster the value of used cars get driven down.

Now when you wanted to buy a new car under the employee pricing plan and needed to trade in a car, you are going to get approximately $1500 less for your trade-in than you would get under normal circumstances. The money you saved from buying under the employee pricing plan was lost on the lowered value on your trade–in. This is a perfect example of the saying "For every action, there is an equal and opposite reaction." This holds true for aggressive pricing campaigns. For every drop in price for new cars also creates a drop in value for used cars.

ODOMETER FRAUD

The National Highway Traffic Safety Administration did a report in April of 2002 that reported that the rate of odometer fraud over the life of a vehicle is approximately 3.47%. That means that there is a 3.47% chance that a vehicle would have its odometer rolled back at any point during the first 11 years of its life. This translates into approximately 452,000 cases of odometer fraud in the United States each year. This costs an average of $2,336 per case of fraud. At 452,000 cases per year, this amounts to $1.056 billion dollars lost each year by consumers. This amount reflects the difference between the inflated prices that consumers actually paid for the rolled-back vehicles and the prices they would have been willing to pay if they had known their true mileage.

In an effort to help this problem, Congress enacted the Truth in Mileage Act of 1986. It requires the seller to disclose the vehicles mileage on the title when ownership is transferred. This applies when a vehicle is sold or leased to auto auctions, car dealerships and individuals. This allows a "paper trail" on each car so this can be detected easier. This is why if you buy or trade in a vehicle at a dealership, you will always sign an odometer statement. This is a legal document that you are signing that attests that the mileage on this form is true. The Truth in Mileage Act hasn't solved the problem but it was the first step in the right direction.

Most cars made nowadays have a digital odometer. Instead of the old rolling style of odometer, they now show up as digital reading on your dashboard when you start your car. Most people think that since the odometer is digital that it can not be altered. That's not true. It isn't like the olden days when you could get a coat hanger under the dashboard and into the odometer and manually roll it back. You also used to be able to plug a drill into the odometer cable and roll the odometer back that way. These are old school tricks that don't work anymore on the newer style odometers. Now it is all done by computer. Cars are now run by computers, and any computer, just like your computer at home, can be altered if someone knows how to do it. **If someone knows how to make it work, then someone knows how to alter it.** There is a chip that controls the odometer which can be removed and reprogrammed to a lower mileage if you know how to do it. It is tougher than the old style of odometers but it is possible. So don't have a false sense of security because the car you are looking at has a digital odometer.

CARFAX REPORTS

The best way as a consumer to detect odometer fraud is the use of a vehicle history service such as CARFAX. This is a service that obtains information from thousands of public and private data sources and puts them into a large database that the general public can access. These sources range from state title and registration records, auto auctions, rental car agencies to police and fire departments. You can use this to see the history on a vehicle which can include the mileage at certain points in the vehicle's life. For example, you can see the reported mileage when the car is inspected, registered or when it is in an accident. This can show you if there is odometer fraud if the last reported entry for the car you are getting a history on has more mileage than it has now or if the mileage has not risen much over the last few entries. Those are some of the tell tale signs that fraud may have occurred.

CARFAX does have its limitations. As of 2004, they have **not** been able to gain information from 23 states. There also can be mistakes in the reporting of information. Since they accept what is given to them by the reporting agencies, there is no way to verify what may have mistakes and what may not. There could also be a lot of missing information due to them not being able to obtain information from 23 states. It also does not contain information on vehicles manufactured prior to 1981. 1981 is when the 17 character VIN number became standard. CARFAX can only process the 17 character VIN numbers when accessing their records.

A car could also have been in accident at the dealer and CARFAX would never have a record of it. The dealer would never have reported it to the authorities which would mean that if the source of information for CARFAX doesn't have it, then CARFAX can't get it. The most common types of damage a car suffers at the dealer are during transportation. The car carriers that transport the cars will arrive from time to time with damage to the cars. It could be from foreign objects that bounced off the road or from objects that they hit during transportation such as low hanging tree branches or street signs hit during turns.

A vehicle could have been in a major accident and it could never show up on a CARFAX report. A car could also be in an accident where they never reported it to the police or their insurance company because they didn't want their insurance rates to go up. This would not show up on a CARFAX report. It also does not show lien release information. That means that a car you buy could have a lien against it that you would need to pay off prior to taking ownership of that car. CARFAX is still a useful source of information, you just need to be aware of the limitations of the service.

FLOOD, SALVAGE AND DAMAGED VEHICLES

One factor you need to be careful with used cars is either flood or salvage vehicles. Flood cars are cars that are totaled in a flood while salvage cars are generally cars that are totaled in some type of accident and then rebuilt and sold again. These cars generally turn up after major flood disasters such as Hurricane Katrina in 2005 where many cars in New Orleans were flooded and totaled by insurance companies. People will buy these cars and bring them to a state where they can either alter the title or forge paperwork so they can get a "clean" title that shows no damage occurred to the car. They then find their way to auctions or private sales and eventually onto dealer's lots. Salvage cars were even reported to be in the market after 9/11. Thousands of cars were damaged or destroyed during 9/11 and some of them were purchased and were put into the market the same way that flood cars are.

The best way to protect yourselves from this scam is to have your own mechanic look at any used car that you are looking to purchase. It will cost you money out of your pocket, but it will be worth it if you buy a lemon by mistake. You may be able to do a preliminary check on a car to see if it is a flood car. The two biggest telltale signs are the pedals and the dashboard. If you look under the dashboard at the brake and accelerator, you would be able to see rust on the top of the pedals where they join the car. Sometimes you can even see leftover sediment or weeds that were in the car during the flood but were never completely cleaned out. If you look at the dashboard you may see a line across it where the water crested or you may also see sediment behind the glass by the gauges. It may be hard to detect as the scam artists work very hard to clean these cars so they don't smell or look dirty so the average person may not notice it. You can also look in the trunk and look at the area where the spare tire is held. There may be sediment in there as well as rust. Look in any area where water can puddle. That is where these signs will show up.

Salvage cars can be detected by looking under the car and looking at the frame. You may see 2 frames welded together to make one, or you may notice that the frame is not straight. You may see a lot of bad paintwork all over the car too. This would be something like overspray on the doors, fenders, headlights or taillights. You are not considered to be an expert at detecting these types of scams, nor am I, which is why bringing the car to an independent mechanic, not one from the dealer, is the best bet to get an honest opinion and vote of confidence from someone you trust. It is well worth the expense.

You are more likely to see salvage or flood cars on a dealer lot that only carries used cars. The reason is that the new car dealers answer to the factory and have contracts with them. Getting involved with illegal behavior is the quickest way to lose a franchise. Therefore, new car dealers tend to stay away from this type of behavior although some still do deal with these types of cars. Some new car dealers can get duped too of they don't pay attention as well. Sometimes salvage or flood vehicles are traded in and the dealer doesn't catch it. So now a lot of car dealers are running a CARFAX on cars that are being traded in with an effort to make sure they do not have issues that they can not see on the outside. The dealers can buy a subscription to CARFAX that allows them to run a large amount of CARFAX reports. They use them not only on cars that are being traded in but also they print them out on the cars on the lot to show customers that the car is clean. Keep in mind that CARFAX has limitations, so a clean report may be clean or it may be missing information that CARFAX does not have access to.

There is one last fact that may surprise you about salvage vehicles. In many states, if a car is a total loss for whatever reason, the insurance company takes control of the title and will "brand" the title as a "salvage" vehicle. This marks the title so anyone else who looks to buy it will be aware that it has been rebuilt. What is interesting is if a car is a total loss, and it is not insured, then the title may never be branded as a salvage vehicle due to an insurance company never taking control of it. The car could be purchased by someone, rebuilt by a body shop even if it has heavy frame or water damage, and then resold to an unwitting person without them ever finding out. The title was never branded and therefore was never marked for any future owners to see. This is a common way to "bypass" the system and sell a car that has been considered a total loss.

Another dirty trick to watch out for is damaged units on the dealer's lot. The unethical car dealer will sell a demo unit as a demo, even though it has been wrecked or had bodywork of some kind performed on it. If you think the demo unit has been wrecked or has been repaired in some way, look for these pointers. Open the hood of the car, check that the screw heads on the hood and body are all painted exactly the same (as they were done by the manufacturer). If you see unpainted screw heads along the painted edge of the car (where the front fenders attach for example) you will want to look further for more signs of fender replacement or bodywork. With the hood still open check the hinges of the hood and the screw heads attaching the hood to the car. Again look for any inconsistencies that suggest body work, hood replacement or paintwork being performed.

There are 2 common inconsistencies that I look for to detect body damage. The first is overspray of paint during the painting process. You can do this several ways but the easiest is to open the doors or hood and look at the door jams, the plastic or rubber around it. Is there paint on it? There shouldn't be when it leaves the factory. There should not be paint on the edges of the headlamps or logos. Those are common places to find overspray, as is any chrome trim. The second inconsistency is to look at the spacing between openings on the vehicle. For example, look at the trunk when it is closed. Is the spacing of the opening on the left the same as on the right? Is one smaller then the other? Is one crooked? The same should be checked on the hood and doors. Look over the roof and see if there are any ripples in it. These are all examples of some bodywork or frame damage that shifted all the parts out of alignment. You probably would not notice this on a test drive but you will notice it as your car gets older or you drive at highway speeds.

I have also seen cars damaged when they are removing them from the car carrier trucks. The driver may release the chains that are holding them on but have not set the emergency brake in the car. Then the car drops off the carrier and onto the ground causing thousands of dollars of damage. A driver may also be careless when backing off the truck and ends up falling off the ramps and damaging the car. The dealer generally fixes it at their body shop and sends the bill to the trucking company. Therefore, there is no reporting of the accident to the police or insurance company so everyone's rates don't go up. A dealer is only required to disclose damage to a new car to the customer when it exceeds 6% of the MSRP. If it is under that then they do not need to disclose it. You could buy a car that has been in an accident and not even know it. With 6% being the threshold, hopefully it should be disclosed to you if major damage was sustained. Some dealers may not disclose it out of fear that the car may never sell.

Damage at dealers also occurs from small traffic accidents on the lot. Cars are parked so close to each other it is inevitable. Damage occurs during snow storms all the time. Plows are generally pretty big and they try to get into small spaces to move snow. It is usually a dangerous combination with cars being hit or sideswiped all the time. Not all cars on a dealer's lot have been in accident, but the car you want may have been in one. So if you buy a new car, don't take it for granted that it is pristine condition. Look over it closely in the daylight and see if anything seems irregular. Most cars have not been in an accident, so just be aware of the possibility.

A dealer is supposed to reveal to the customer that car is damaged once it has damage that exceeds 6% of the sale price. Some dealers follow this, while others do not. Also, dealers can fix their own cars for cheaper than you can get one fixed. So that 6% figure may not be reached as easy as you think. Look every car over for these little tips for damage. Just because it is new does not mean it is perfect.

FACTORY CERTIFIED USED CARS

The newest programs that are helping the sale of used cars are "Factory Certified" programs. These programs take used cars that qualify for certification which are usually low mileage late model cars that haven't been in a major accident or had any major mechanical issues. A lot of these cars are off lease cars that fit the profile of what the factory is looking for. What the dealer does is put these cars through an in depth inspection such as a 150 point inspection of the mechanical, electrical and mechanical items. These items must meet factory standards or they must be replaced. Some items might be tires that must meet minimum tread depth, windshield wiper quality, transmission, radio, amongst several other items. Each factory has different standards and varies in the number of points that are checked on the car. The inspection itself is much more comprehensive than what a normal used car goes through.

Once the car passes that and is brought up to the standard set by the factory, it is sold as a "Factory Certified" car. What that gets you is usually an extension of the warranty. It usually consists of extending the full factory warranty by one year and then they give you powertrain coverage up to 100,000 miles. Each manufacturer's program is different in what they offer but they are all very similar. The dealer also can offer an extended warranty that will cover the car once the factory warranty runs out. It usually upgrades the powertrain coverage up to bumper to bumper coverage. This warranty is usually pretty cheap compared to buying the same coverage when the car is brand new. These warranty upgrades can cost the dealer any where from a few hundred dollars to about $1200 dollars depending on the cost and model of the car. Luxury or high-end vehicles usually cost more. The dealer usually tries to mark them up at least $500 when they sell them.

The dealer will also try to charge more for a certified car rather than one that is non-certified. This is usually because they need to spend more in the service department to bring the car up to factory standards as well as purchasing the certification from the factory. If do you some shopping around, you can find some similar cars to compare prices. This way you can get quotes from dealers and shop around and have them compete for your business. This can be handled the same way you would when buying a new car. The difference here is that every dealer has paid different amounts for their used cars. Two dealers may have the exact same car but one may own it for $1000 less because of how they bought it (trade-in, auction, etc.) or how much they spend to bring the car up to standard. One dealer may give you a better deal than another because they own the car for a cheaper price. So you still can find a good deal, you just may need to look a little harder or longer. Just because a car is or isn't certified makes no difference in your ability to get a good deal.

You will also notice during your shopping that the foreign manufacturers have a better certification program than the domestic manufacturers. Their certification warranty coverage and length are generally better than the domestics. Their inspection is also more in depth and the standards are higher. It also helps that used foreign cars hold their value better than domestic cars which helps the used car sales for the foreign car dealers. Of all my experience, I found the manufacturers with the best certification programs are Toyota and Honda. They have the most in-depth program with the best warranty coverage.

BUYING A CAR BY EMAIL

A great deal of people feel they can get buy a car and get a good deal by emailing a dealership. This could not be farther from the truth. Many dealers have finally grasped the internet and realized that it is another source of business. Although, dealers still are not handing their Internet business to the best of their ability. Some larger dealers can afford to have a Business Development Center which can handle all of the internet business. Not all dealers can afford to have one, so most go without and settle for an "Internet Salesperson." This is usually one person who handles of the emails and sends prices out all over the internet to customers who request them.

I was asked by a friend to help him buy a new car. He knew exactly what he wanted but he traveled all the time and was not home enough to go through the process. I took this as opportunity to try to see how far I would get on the internet. I emailed every dealer within 100 miles that sold the car he wanted. Some dealers had a nice auto reply feature that sent me back an informative email telling me about the dealer and that someone would respond to me shortly. Of the 11 dealers I contacted only 7 responded to my email. 4 of those 7 took more than 24 hours to get back to me. Of the 3 that got back within 3-4 hours, 2 were ready to work with me while 1 said, "You live too far from me. You should buy your car closer to home." That one threw me for a loop. He obviously had no clue my friend was willing to drive the 75 miles to this dealer if the price was right. The other 2 responses wanted to set an appointment up with me to come into the dealership and check out their inventory. They would not give me their best price as I had asked. It took me several emails over a couple of days to finally get some numbers out of them. Some even wrote that they will beat any price out there. Then I got a response from one that told me I would get a better price if I came into the showroom. Apparently there must be 2 prices. One price for people who are outside the showroom, and one for who are inside. It didn't make sense but was part of the game I expected. Their goal is to get you in the showroom so they can control you. The dealer knows that as long as you are in their showroom, you are not shopping somewhere else.

Of the 7 that finally responded, they all eventually gave me prices but they were evasive about all the questions I had, such as documentation fees or accessory pricing. Some dealers did give me a very good price but one dealer gave me a price that was much lower than the others. I felt that this was a "bait and switch" by the dealer to get me in the door and then tell me "That price was for a different model, we made a mistake." Then once I was there, they would get me to purchase the car I wanted at a higher price. Eventually I got a competitive price from the local dealer in my friend's town and he ended up buying from that dealer. The only issue was that we had to show them the quotes from the other dealers. It forced them to drop $2000 from their original price that they quoted me in order to get the deal.

The moral of the story is this. Buying your car over the internet can be time consuming. Response time is generally poor, even from the biggest and best dealers. You also may not get a response from certain dealers as they do not have a good system set up to handle those inquiries. Anyone responding to your email inquiry will have a sole purpose of setting up an appointment to come into the dealer. By using email, they can write back to you as much, or as little, as they want. On the phone, if you ask them a question, they need to answer it immediately. By email, they can tell you everything that you want to hear as long as it gets you in the showroom where they have more control of you. I didn't find it to be an effective way to purchase a car. Using the phone would have allowed me to have all of my prices and questions answered within one day rather than over a course of a week. My system is much more effective than using the internet. You will realize that as I share more information with you as you read more of this book.

BUYING FROM RENTAL CAR COMPANIES

A lot of rental car companies sell their cars to car dealers around the country. Some of them even have their own dealers. Some people also feel that these are the type of cars that they don't want to buy. Believe it or not, these are actually some of the better cars to buy. The reason is that they are taken care of very well. Rental car companies usually do all the regularly scheduled maintenance on their cars. They also put them through an inspection and cleaning after every time they are turned in by a customer. They are also only kept in their fleet for only a year or two at the longest. So they get to the dealership with average miles and are only a year or two old. The only rental cars that you should be concerned about are sports cars. People may treat them with a little less respect when they rent them, but the rental car company still takes pretty good care of them overall. I have worked with many rental car companies and they know when a car has been abused as does the dealer. Sports cars are known to be abused more than other cars. Dealers are very likely to stay away from those types of cars because they know that.

A good inspection by your mechanic would bring out any concerns that you should have about the car such as wear and tear items and signs of accidents or abuse. The best cars come from the more respectable rental car companies such as Hertz, Avis, Enterprise, Alamo or Dollar. They tend to spend more money keeping their fleet running and up to date with maintenance.

GOVERNMENT AUCTIONS

Every once and a while you see and advertisement on TV for cars you can buy at a government auctions for some crazy amount like $99/month or thousands below retail value. They are usually drug forfeitures or government vehicles that are being sold to make money for the state. The problem is actually finding the deals that they talk about on the advertising.

First of all, any good quality vehicles are usually purchased by people that work for the government as they sometimes are given first crack at purchasing the vehicles. The luxury or sports cars are sometimes kept and used by undercover police drug units.

Second, you used to be able to find good deals when not many people knew about these auctions. Therefore, you would have very little competition and would actually be able to get a good deal. Now they advertise them more with the help of the internet and television. So now you have a lot more people showing up hoping to get a good deal. Since everyone else wants the cars too, you will not pay much below retail value, which is no better a deal then you could get at a car dealer.

Third and finally, most of the vehicles either don't run, do not have ignition keys or both. So once you buy them, you need to find a way to start them and then get a new ignition system or get a new key made. Neither of which is cheap. The vehicles are all usually sold "as is." So you buy them as you see them. If you drive it off the lot and the engine dies as you pull out of the lot, you are out of luck. There is no recourse against the auction or the government. These auctions are generally not a good place to get a good car or a good deal. It sounds great when they advertise it, but the deals are truly few and far between.

WHOLESALE AUCTIONS

Wholesale auctions are the most popular source of cars for dealers. Most of their used car inventory comes from the auctions. Most auctions are for licensed dealers only so the normal everyday consumer does not usually have access to these. However, there are also auctions that are open to the general public. Some dealers actually host them at their dealership. There are opportunities to get a good deal there, but you need to be on your toes. First of all, you need to know what you are looking at. What type of car and what trim level is it? What does it have for options? What is the book value? How many miles does it have? Does it have signs of being in an accident? What problems are recurrent in that model that you need to look for? All of these questions are important and are commonly known by most dealers at an auction. They are good at it because they see thousands of cars a year go through the auction blocks. For the regular consumer, this is a pretty heavy task. There is a lot to know. Plus you need to get there early if they give you the opportunity the test drive the car around the parking lot. But, you really can't get a good feel for a car by driving it around the lot.

Another issue at the auction is knowing how to bid. If they use professional auctioneers then you will probably not be able to understand what they are saying. They speak very quickly and unless you listen to them regularly, you may not be able to make out what numbers they are actually saying. Plus you need to know the tricks they play. The dealer who is selling the car is usually up on the block with the auctioneer as his cars go through the lane. The dealer wants the most amount of money for his car as possible. So what the auctioneer will do is make bids that don't exist. What that means is that you may be bidding on a car and he sees that you want it. In order to get the price up higher and have people gain interest, the auctioneer will take your bid and then make it look like someone behind you has bid the car higher so you will come back and bid again. Therefore, the bids go higher and the buyer overpays for the car and the dealer makes out with a good price. You don't know this is going on because the "ghost bidder" is behind you and you usually don't look and check to see who is bidding behind you as you are paying attention to the auctioneer and the car. Plus the cars are going through the lane pretty quick. Things move very quickly and are hard to keep up with. This where your lack of experience can get you in trouble and cause you to get a bad deal. The auctioneer also gets paid on how many cars get sold. So it is in the auctioneer's best interest to get every car sold no matter what.

Auctions are also a hard place to really get an idea what type of car you are getting. It may look alright on the outside but there could be underlying problems that you don't know about. It could have a rolled back odometer, a bad transmission, or structural damage. Most of the dealer auctions have rules that allow a vehicle with those problems to be returned to dealer who sold it and get a full refund. If you use an auction that is open to the public, make sure there is protection for the buyer in case you are a victim of fraud. If they don't have any provisions in place for that, then you should not buy a car there because you may get taken for a ride.

You may still be better off buying from a dealer because they have the ability to know what type of car they are buying and the ability to fix whatever is wrong with the car relatively easy. For the normal consumer there may be too much of a chance to get a lemon. Keep in mind, the better cars will go to the dealer auction because the dealers can tell if the cars are a lemon. Consumers are not that savvy so the lesser quality cars may end up at an auction that is open to the public. If you really need a used car that is not on the lot at your favorite dealer, then they usually have the ability to go to the auction and try to buy one that you may want. That may be a better route than trying to go to an auction yourself and be taken advantage of.

eBay Motors is also a good website to buy or sell your car. The best part about eBay is that it can show a great deal of information about the car in both facts and pictures. The more you see and know about a car, the more comfortable you are. They also show the VIN number so you can run a CARFAX if you want to. A lot of people who sell on eBay will allow you to test drive the car if you wish. This obviously is only possible if you are looking at a car that is relatively close to you. This service is nationwide so you may find a car you like but it may be half way across the country. You may be able to get a good deal on eBay, but you are more likely to get a car that you really want rather than a good deal. You really don't know the history of the car that you are buying nor do you have any recourse if there is an issue after the fact. This is a good service, but your protection is limited. A private buyer also may not be as willing to do anything to the car to bring it up to snuff as a dealer might be.

BUYING FROM A WHOLESALE CLUB

There are several wholesale suppliers that offer discount auto purchase plans. The most popular ones that I have seen is Costco, Sam's Club and BJ's Wholesale Club. While these are all reputable business, the discount programs they offer are not what you think. You are not buying the car from that store. You are still buying it from the dealership. How this works is simple. The local store contracts with the local car dealer or several different car dealers who will take turns displaying their vehicle at the store, usually by the main entrance, so they can get the most attention. On the window of this car will be the normal window sticker but there will be some paperwork on the window or somewhere where you can contact the dealer or a person at the dealership who handles this "program." This is to create an illusion that this program is for "special" people who belong to the wholesale club.

This program is really designed to increase traffic for the dealer and get their name out in the public to help boost sales. The price they get from the dealer is not necessarily the best price, but it is still a good price. The illusion the dealer creates is that you are getting a price that nobody else can get except members in that program. It helps relieve some of the hassle that many people dislike when they go to the dealership to purchase a car. I have seen many people contact my dealerships through this program. There was not a great deal of sales that were generated from it, although it did get our name out there and was able to give us some traffic in the dealership. Overall, I found the prices that they received were no better than if they walked in the door and negotiated a good deal. These programs are more for marketing purposes. They are not bad programs, they just may not be as good as you think they are.

The same rings true for car financing offers through the same clubs. These programs also are run by outside finance companies. I have seen many customers come in with checks from these companies and have found out that the rates they are charging their customer were not always the best. Most times I could have obtained a better rate from my bank than they received from theirs. One customer thought that it must be the best rate since it was from their "wholesale club." When they found out it wasn't the best they were upset and felt they were mislead. **In cases like this, it is all about the appearance of getting a good deal.** In most cases, the deal you get is not the deal you think you are getting.

BUYING A USED CAR FROM A USED CAR DEALER OR A NEW CAR DEALER

If you are going to buy a used car from a dealer then you need to determine which type of dealer you will buy from. Are going to buy your used car from a new car dealer or a used car dealer? Some people don't think that there is a difference. The difference is actually pretty big. **A new car dealer will generally give you better service and a lot of times a better inventory.** It is usually lower mileage and late model cars. A new car dealer can also sell certified used cars through the manufacturer program. For example, a Honda dealer can sell a factory certified used car. A used car dealer does not have that ability. A new car dealer will also be less likely to sell a fraudulent car since any involvement with fraudulent cars could effect their franchise agreement with the factory. They could lose their franchise which could put some dealers out of business as the franchise it what gives a dealer their legitimacy. So a dealer will do everything they can not to destroy that relationship with the factory. They also would have the factory certified technicians to work on their used cars. So that same Honda we discussed earlier would be worked on by a factory certified Honda technician.

A used car dealer, however, may have a wide variety of makes and models on their lot. These cars will be worked on by a mechanic who probably is not certified by any factory and specializes in no particular model. So he could be a jack of all trades, master of none. He may not be aware of certain inherent problems in some models that he needs to look for when inspecting a car to get it ready for sale on the lot. A used car dealer may also have cars that are older and have higher miles. This is because they attract a customer that usually wants to spend a lot less than they would at a new car dealer. So the older high mileage cars are in their inventory to satisfy those customers. They also may push the envelope with fraudulent or heavily damaged cars since they don't have a franchise or manufacturer to deal with or answer to. They could still lose their dealer license if they commit fraudulent acts, but they don't have the risk of losing a new car franchise.

If you try to purchase a used car from a used car dealer, you may want to be aware of what other types of cars they sell. For example, if you are looking to buy a BMW for $25,000-$30,000 from a dealer that specializes in Buick and Pontiacs that cost between $8,000-$13,000, then you may want to be wary. That dealer may not be able to handle the issues that the BMW may have when it comes into the dealer. The mechanics will not be as familiar with the issues of that vehicle. A used car dealer that specializes in highline used cars such as BMW's may not have any problems in getting the car ready for purchase. If you bring that BMW back to the Buick/Pontiac dealer for an issue after delivery, they may just tell you to bring it to a BMW dealer as they would not know how to diagnose or fix your problem. After all, BMW's are not their specialty. A highline used car store will have experience with those brands and be able to diagnose and fix your problems relatively easy due to their experience with the brand. The same works in reverse too. Buying a Buick or Pontiac from a dealer that sells mostly BMW's should make you worry too.

A used car dealer may also try to sell a "certified" car. What those cars usually entail is the dealer putting some type of warranty on it and calling it "certified." This way the used car dealer makes the customer think that they are getting the same certification that they could get at a new car dealer. That is far from the truth. If you want to get a better quality car with a good certification program and lessen your chance of getting a fraudulent car, then a buying a used car at a new car dealer will be your best bet.

Another sales tactic that dealers tend to use is to use a different book when telling you the book value of the car that you are buying. For example, a used car may have a window sticker on it that the dealer has put on. This sticker may have the options listed as well as the mileage and any other pertinent information. But what is more important is that the dealer may have the price on it and will also include the "Blue Book Value" on it in order to show how much money you are saving.

Here is how it may look:

Blue Book Value: **$15,000**
Our Sale Price **$13,500**

Upon first look you may think you are saving $1500 when buying at this price. The problem here is that Kelley Blue Book is known as a higher value book. It is known more as a West Coast book. It is used to more to determine values on the West Coast which tend to hold their value better because they aren't exposed to weather elements as they are in other parts of the country. What the dealer is doing is using an inflated value of the car to show it is priced well below its actual value. They may use Kelley Blue Book to show how much their car is worth, but they won't use Kelley Blue Book when determining the value of your car when you trade it in. It is just a way that the dealer presents their car to make it look like you are getting a good deal. In reality you are not. If the dealer still thinks this is legitimate way of determining the value of their car, then ask them to use Kelley Blue Book when determining the value of your trade. Chances are that they will not. It is just another way for the dealer to put lipstick on a pig.

chapter six

SECRETS YOU MAY NEVER HAVE KNOWN ABOUT

THE HIDDEN COST OF PAYING CASH

not everyone that buys a car finances it. Some customers pay cash. You may think that this is great because you don't have any car payments. This may sound great for some people, but it may not be a smart investment for others. Some people that are paying cash may even be making a bad investment.

Some people will pay cash for a car but only own the car for a few years. They like to have the latest and greatest car that is available. This is great and is very common among cash buyers. If you pay cash for a car and keep it for a long time or until it is no longer useful, then paying cash may be good alternative. If you plan on trading in your car every few years, then there may be an option that is more economically sound. There is something that most manufacturers

167

offer that most people don't know about. It's called a "One Pay Lease." This is still a lease just as any other lease, but instead of making payments each month, you make one large payment at the beginning and never make one again for the life of the lease.

What makes this a good alternative? Well, for starters your car that you trade in to a dealer in a few years will be worth about 30-40% of its value. If you paid $20,000 for that car then it may be worth about $6,000 to $8,000 after a few years, but you haven't used 60-70% of the value of your car. Your car still has plenty of years left in it, probably well in excess of 10 years if you take good care of it. In a one pay lease, you will pay for the use of the car for the 3 years or whatever term you take, rather than pay for the full value of the vehicle and take a bath on what it is worth when you trade it in. The residual value would be probably 50% or higher. What you would pay out of pocket, including interest, will still be less than the difference between what you paid and what you received when you traded the car in. You could save thousands of dollars by taking this route. And best of all, you still get a new car every few years.

Example:

	One pay lease:	Cash:
Purchase price:	$20,000	$20,000
Length owned:	3 years	3 years
Residual Value:	$12,000	N/A
Trade-in Value:	N/A	$8,000
Money spent:	$8,000	$12,000
Interest paid:	$2,000	$0
Total Expense:	**$10,000**	**$12,000**

So you can see, even though you paid interest on the lease, your total expenses were $2,000 less. Sometimes a one pay lease isn't that advantageous as some cars don't lease as well as others, but you can see that you do save money in the long run. So before you decide to pay cash for a car, do some math and see if you can save money by doing a one-pay lease instead. This is one of the "hidden costs of paying cash."

Sometimes financing is also cheaper than paying cash. This may also sound odd but like I said before, there is a "hidden cost to paying cash." You can finance a $20,000 car and pay less in interest than you would gain in interest earned on an investment account such as a bank CD or mutual fund. For example, if you took your $20,000 and invested in a CD or other investment account with a 4% rate of return, you would actually make more money than financing the $20,000 from a bank at rate of 5%.

Example

Financing:

> Loan amount: $20,000
>
> Interest Rate: 5%
>
> Term: 5 years
>
> Monthly payment: $377
>
> Interest paid: $2645
>
> **Total amount out of pocket: $22,645**

Investing:

Investment: $20,000

Term: 5 years

Rate of return: 4%

Interest Earned: $4333

Total amount after interest earned: $24,333

As you can see from both examples, if you choose to invest the money you would have spent on the car and financed it instead, you would have a net gain of about $1688. **That $1688 is the "hidden cost of paying cash."** This is the amount you may lose if you paid cash for a car using this scenario. This is still the case even though your interest rate on the loan is greater than the rate of return on your investment account. The reason is because the interest on your loan is decreasing as your balance goes down. On your investment account, your interest earned is going up over time because your interest is also gaining interest. It is compounding interest which means that it gains money on itself over time. As the balance grows, the amount that is earning interest also grows. This is one of the hardest concepts for a customer to understand because they feel having no payments is the best part of paying cash. They just need to be shown this example to understand how advantageous this can be. The only thing you need to remember with this scenario is that you need to have the ability to make the monthly payments while your money is invested. It usually isn't a problem for most people, but if you do not have an income then this may not work for you. Check with your accountant and financial advisor to be sure if this works for you.

BAD CREDIT

Bad credit can be defined a few different ways. A lot of people think that bad credit has to do with your credit score. It has something to do with your credit score but there are a lot of other factors that come into play when determining your credit rating. It includes your credit score but also uses other factors such as late payments, amount of debt, time on your job, time living at your residence, amount of jobs in last 2 years and type of job held as well as credit card debt.

The longer you have been working at the same job, the longer you have been at your residence, the lower the amount of late payments and the fewer amounts of jobs that you have held in the last 2 years can help your credit risk to the banks. If you have the opposite, then your risk is high to the bank and your credit score may suffer and lessen your ability to get a loan or one with a good rate.

What credit score is bad? Well, score doesn't define whether you are good or bad. You may have a FICO score of 620 but it may be a "good" 620 which means that you have good time on the job and good time at your residence but you may have a few late payments and some credit card debt. Then there are people with a "bad" 620 which mean that they have very little credit card debt, several late payments and little time on the job at their residence. The "good" 620 score is more likely to get a loan than a "bad" 620 score. This just shows that you can't look at credit score alone. Although, it would be better to be higher than a 620 score in order to not have to run into problems when trying to finance a car.

Many people think that since they have bad credit that they are all alone and can't buy a car. **Truth be told, a large amount of the American public have credit issues.** These issues can be late payments, collections, high debt load, bankruptcies and even repossessions. The dealers all know this. The dealers refer to this as "sub-prime credit." They train their Business Managers to deal with this type of customer. The reason why they do that is because dealing with this type of credit challenged customer can be very lucrative for a dealer. The dealers usually have several sources for getting financing for people with credit issues, while the customer may only have one or two sources such as their local bank or credit union. So they tend to be at the mercy of the dealer because they feel that nobody else can get them a loan. Or at least that is what they want you to believe.

The reason why this type of customer is lucrative for a dealer is because once they get them financed, they mark up everything as much as they can and then present it in a light that makes it sound like that they have no choice but to accept it. What they will do is take your loan that they get you, add on as many points to the loan rate as the bank allows, stretch the finance term out as much as the bank will approve for them, mark up the warranty as much as the bank allows and any other products that bank will approve the customer for. And of course they do everything in their power for you to get excited about this car so you take mental ownership. They let you drive it as long as you want. They tell you how great you look in the car. They tell you how everyone will love your car. This way you get so excited about the car that you will pay anything for it. You are like putty in their hands.

Some larger dealers have an entire department of Business Managers dedicated just to sub-prime financing. They are highly trained on how to manhandle a sub-prime customer and maximize every bit of profit that is available to them. Their job not only is to get someone financed with bad credit, but to fleece them of every penny they have. They give so much business to this type of bank that they can get more people loans due to that large amount of business. Then they add in every product that the bank allows at the most amount of markup possible. Finally, they present it to the customer in a way where they feel that you have no choice but to take it because of their credit situation. From this they make the customer feel so bad about themselves and so guilty that they did so much work for them that they feel that don't have choice but to sign all the paperwork. This is exactly why I recommend finding your own financing. You can save yourself thousands of dollars and choose a car more to your liking rather than what the dealer wants you to buy. I'm sure you would rather save thousands of dollars than spend it. Don't let them tell you what you can buy. Tell them what you want.

Against popular belief, there is a way to protect you against this happening. There are a few sources, besides your local bank or credit union, which can help you get financed. From my experience I have seen 3 finance sources that help people with credit issues get financed without having to go through the dealer. The three sources are Capital One Auto Finance, Household Auto Finance (HSBC) and E-Loan. I found that these sources tend to be more forgiving than most banks, plus you don't have to worry about the rate being marked up or any fees being charged to you like the dealer would. They may request certain items from you such as pay stubs or a utility bill as a proof of residency. You already know what you qualify for before you enter the dealership. You have an idea of what your payment is and how much you can spend on a car. There are no hidden surprises like if you financed at the dealer. The difference is that you are going to the same banks that they use and cutting out the middle man which saves you money.

Beware that there are several banks on the internet that claim to help people with bad credit. The problem is that some of these companies may be "fly by night" operations. They are not always licensed to do business in most states. A lot of dealers may not accept checks from these companies because of fear that the checks may be no good. The dealer's biggest concern is making sure they get paid by the bank. These problem banks have made a living off of issuing checks that are no good. So please be aware of them and try to stick with the banks that I recommended.

What these banks that I recommended will usually do is send you something they call a "draft note" or a "bank draft." That basically means that they send you a blank check to fill out at the dealership. This is treated as a check and then the dealer submits it to the bank as any other check. The bank may allow you to purchase an extended warranty but not much else. In some cases you may not even be allowed to purchase any extra products. It all depends on your credit situation. Sometimes the bank will give you a pre-approval letter to bring to the dealer. In this case, the letter will tell you the specifics about the approval but the only difference are that the dealer will have to prepare the paperwork. The dealer doesn't make any money, in fact they may have to pay a fee to the bank for the referral to the dealer. Just check the purchase and sale agreement to make sure it matches the finance contract. This is when the dealer may try to add in the referral fee to your sale price so they don't have to pay it. Keep an eye on it to make sure the dealer doesn't try to slide it in without you knowing it.

There is one thing you need to be aware of when dealing with sub-prime finance banks. They are very strict with the advance that they will give you. Your advance is the percentage of the value of the car that they will allow you to borrow. For example, if the bank will allow you 90% of the retail book value of a car, then that would mean that if you are looking at a car that is valued at $20,000, then the most you can loan on that car is $18,000. If you are trading in a car then you should not owe more than it is worth because that difference will be added into the loan. On a new car, the banks will usually go by invoice price when they are figuring your advance but on used cars they tend to use either retail or trade value as listed in the NADA guide. Your credit will determine that advance. Some may qualify for over 100% while others may qualify for less.

What a lot of dealers will do to sub-prime customers is try to lead them into a certain car. Because of all the different factors that go into getting financing for you, they will say that because of these extenuating circumstances that you will only qualify for a certain car on the lot. It may be true that only some cars will qualify for financing under your program, but what the dealer won't tell you is that you may qualify for a few or several vehicles. The reason why they do this is that they usually want to get rid of an older car or one that nobody else wants to buy because of the color or options. So they tell you that this is the only one you qualify for so you think that you have no choice. Don't be afraid to look at other vehicles on the lot, especially if you really don't like the car. Other people are not buying that car for a reason too.

In most circumstances a sub-prime customer will qualify for a used car. The reason is because used cars are usually sold under book value which will help if the bank only allows you a certain amount to finance or if they limit the advance allowed on a car. Plus most sub-prime customers are usually trading in a car that they owe more on than it is worth. A used car is the best opportunity to fit that amount into the loan and still be within bank guidelines. Keep in mind that because of your credit, you may not be able to afford the luxury car or truck that you had dreamed of. Your best bet is to find a nice used car that is cheaper than a new one and finance less than you are approved for. The reason being is that a lot of people will buy a car for the maximum allowed by the bank but end up getting in trouble down the line because they never figured on their insurance or gas bills going up. Therefore, the payment gets to be too much to handle when you add the ancillary costs that go with owning a car. This can spiral into a bad situation where your credit gets even worse and you are never able to fix your credit.

Keep in mind as well that just because you have bad credit does not mean that you can not qualify for special financing. There are times when a manufacturer will really need to move some inventory off the dealer's lots. What they will do is put pressure on their finance company (GMAC, Toyota Motor Credit, American Honda Finance, etc.) to be a little more lenient with their lending policies. This allows the dealers to get more people approved so they can sell more cars and clear out their inventory. You may even be able to buy a new car and get special financing or regular financing without paying a high rate like you would if you went through a sub-prime finance company. This happens from time to time, usually at the end of a model year when they are trying to get rid of last years models in order to make way for the new ones. But it could happen during slow times of the year as well such as the winter time. A lot of the manufacturer's finance companies will allow you to apply online and get approved. This way you may get to know what rate you are approved for plus you now know that you actually are approved.

HOW TO FIX YOUR CREDIT

Since your credit score does affect your loan rates, you need to be aware of how to raise it. The higher your score, the better your rates will be. These tips should help you get your score up by simply changing some of your spending habits and money management skills.

Fixing your credit or raising your score can be a tricky issue. Everyone has an opinion of how it should be done. After doing research on your FICO score and how it is determined, I've come up with these helpful tips to help you improve your credit score. I am not a financial advisor, but this information was obtained from information obtained from FICO, the Fair Isaac Corporation, which is the company that determines your credit score. In order to improve your score you need to follow all of these recommendations, not just a few of them. It may sound hard to some people, but it really is simply all about adjusting your spending habits into a system that works by using these tips.

1. **Pay your bills on time**. It's never too late to start. Even if you've had serious delinquencies in the past, they will count less over time.

2. **Keep credit cards balances low**. High outstanding debt can pull down your score. The secret to not having credit card balances affect your

credit is to keep your credit card balances under 50% of your approved amount on **each** card. For example, if your card has a $1000 limit, then your balance should be under $500 at all times. I recommend people keep their balance at 40% or less in case you spend too much one month. Your credit score will take a hit once you reach 50% of your limit. It will take another hit when you reach 75% of your limit. This is the biggest cause of people lowering their score besides late payments.

3. **Don't open new credit card accounts you don't need.** This approach could backfire and actually lower your score.

4. **Pay off debt rather than moving it around**. The most effective way to improve your score is by simply paying down the amount you owe.

5. **Have credit cards - but manage them responsibly.** In general, having credit cards and installment loans which you pay on time will raise your score.

6. **Don't open multiple accounts too quickly especially if you have a short credit history.** This can look risky because you are taking on a lot of possible debt. New accounts will also lower the average age of your existing accounts, something that your FICO score also considers.

7. **Don't close an account to remove it from your record.** Closed accounts will still show up on your credit and may be considered by the score. In fact, closing accounts can sometimes hurt your score unless you also pay down your debt at the same time.

8. **Check your report for accuracy.** Clear up any inaccurate information by contacting all three credit bureaus. Requesting a copy or your credit report won't affect your score if you order it directly from the credit reporting agency.

9. **Shop for a loan within a focused period of time.** FICO scores distinguish between a search for a single loan and a search for many new credit lines, based in part on the length of time over which recent requests for credit occur.

There are a lot of people or companies out there that claim to be able to help people with credit issues or debt. Debt consolidation or debt counseling services are the most popular, but there are drawbacks to going through one. They will negotiate with your debtors to try to get them to lower your balance owed or your interest rate. Then they consolidate it into one payment that you make to them which is usually lower than what you were paying before.

The problem is that while you are in debt counseling, a lot of banks will not give you a loan until you are out. Some people can be in counseling for a few years. Plus, these services are doing things that you could do on your own but they just are better skilled at it. You could call your credit card companies and negotiate a lower balance or rate if you wanted to. The difference is that some of the interest and balance that they negotiate down they may keep to themselves. Plus they charge you a fee to do it. And then some may even do nothing that they promise you or they may require that you purchase their "educational kit" to teach you how to you improve your credit. That kit may cost more than this book, and this book has a whole lot more information plus tips on how to improve your credit.

There are also companies out there that claim to be able to fix your bad credit. This is misleading at the least. First of all, you can't fix bad credit that is already on your credit bureau, unless it is a mistake by the company that reported it. If you didn't really pay a bill, then it will show up as a delinquency on your credit. These companies will tell you that they can fix your credit even if you have had a bankruptcy or other serious delinquencies.

What they actually do is look at your credit bureau and see what you have for credit issues. These agencies are familiar with the credit reporting laws and just apply them to your situation. They will send letters to all the creditors that are showing late payments and collections. What they do in these letters is demand that the creditors prove that your payments are in fact late or that certain accounts are in collection. If they don't respond within 30 days then the creditors are required to remove it from your credit bureau. Most of the large credit card companies don't respond within 30 days because they are very large and can't handle the request quick enough. So the items in question will be removed and your credit score goes up quickly. The problem is that after a month or so, when the companies get back to the agency and verify that the delinquencies are true, then they go back on your credit bureau and your score drops back down again. So this may raise your score temporarily, but it won't raise it for the long term. Only good spending habits and money management can do that. To make matters worse they may charge you several hundred to over a thousand dollars in order to perform this "temporary fix."

BUT HERE, PAY HERE

Watch out for dealers that push you into a "Buy Here, Pay Here" situation. This is for people who either have bad credit or no credit or can't finance a car under normal circumstances. Basically what a dealer does is rent a used car to the customer. Every week they come into the dealer and pay for the car. That is where the term "Buy Here, Pay Here" come from. They buy it, or rent it in this case, at the dealer and then they pay for it at the dealer too. The customer never ends up owning the car nor do they gain any credit history in most cases. Some programs will allow you to buy the car down the road but the rate will be through the roof. A lot of programs out there will allow the dealer to get you a car loan if you have paid the dealer on time for a year or two. This works if the dealer keeps legitimate records on your payment history. Basically they wait until you have enough credit history in order to get financing. This is common with young people who generally don't know enough about the process of buying a car. This process is not recommended as it is very profitable for the dealer and is a bad investment for the customer.

"NO HAGGLE" OR "ONE PRICE" DEALERS

The newest fad with dealers is that they call themselves "no haggle" dealers. You may also see it as "one price" or a "no dicker sticker" store. This means that they give you the lowest price up front so you don't have to go through the negotiation process and feel you were taken advantage of because you don't know how to negotiate. The dealers love this because it attracts customers who are somewhat afraid to go into a car dealership and buy a car. This no haggle pricing is getting so popular that manufacturers themselves are turning to that type of selling. Their dealers are required to follow the no haggle policy as part of their dealer agreement. The two most popular no haggle manufacturers are Saturn and Scion.

The only problem with this type of pricing is with most dealers the "no haggle" price that is posted on the car is not really the best price. **It is the price**

that the dealer wants to charge with a comfortable amount of profit figured in. Most customers think it is the best price because it is the "no haggle" price. That usually is far from the truth. I have only seen a few dealers who truly have a "no haggle" price that is the best price around. These dealers are usually very large and sell upwards of 500 cars a month. Their entire goal is to sell the most amounts of cars possible with very little profit. They may not make much profit on each car but if you take that little bit of profit and multiply it by over 500 cars a month, then it all adds up. Plus, they will make money in the finance office that far outweighs the profit made on the car itself.

For smaller dealers who sell less, the no haggle price is generally set at a price where the profit margin is comfortable for the dealer. But what the customer doesn't know is that the no haggle price really can be haggled. I have worked at "one price, no haggle" dealers where the set price really wasn't adhered to. If a customer came in and had a better price from another dealer then we would lower our price in order to get the deal from the customer. This process just defeated the purpose of the "no haggle" price. Most customers think that this doesn't happen, but it actually happens very often. The dealer will move from the set price if they feel it isn't good enough.

If you shop around and run into a one price dealer, you can still follow the same process as I set out in this book, you just need to let the "no haggle" salesman know that if you find a better price, you will buy from that dealership. Some may lower the price, and some may not. If you still find a better price, then you can still go back to them to see if they can beat the price quote that you have. They may still give you a better price when they realize what they are up against. You can look at a "no haggle" price and think to yourself, "The no haggle price is for people who don't know how to negotiate. The price I'll get is better because I have more information than them from reading this book."

In other words, don't be afraid of a "no haggle" dealer. They are just like all the other dealers except they are just using a different pricing strategy in order to attract more customers.

Some manufacturers are going to a one price strategy as an entire company. Saturn was one of the first with Scion coming into the game recently. Both are one price dealers with some subtle differences. Scion not only has one price for the cars, but they have one price financing, one price warranties, one price accessories, etc. Saturn, which is made by General Motors, does not have set pricing on anything other than the car. The only problem is that the "no haggle" price for Saturn is usually the MSRP. So what good is a "no haggle" or a "one price" store if there is no discount on the price? It is just the way they present it that makes it look so good. They treat the customer with a more respect than the average customer which goes a long way towards making a sale. This is exactly why most Saturn dealers are very profitable, even more than the other lines made by GM in some cases. This also is because they make a lot of money in the finance office because there is no set pricing on their products as there are in Scion. The best part about Saturn is that you can still shop around and get a price below the "no haggle" price. The dealers will work with you if you get a better price. They want your business and will do what it takes to earn it.

Scion is a relatively new brand that was introduced by Toyota. It was designed with a target market of the younger generation who want to customize their cars or buy something affordable yet sporty or useful. They succeeded in that because of the pricing and financing strategy. But what they don't tell you is you may qualify for better finance rates at local banks or credit unions. By doing that you may still be able to take advantage of all the rebates plus get a good rate from your own bank. If you are looking to purchase some additional or aftermarket parts, you may also be able to get the same parts from parts stores outside the dealership for a cheaper price. If you shop around you may get dealers to compete for your business by giving you a lower price, for both the car and the additional parts, from another dealer as well. The factory may not want them to do it, but when it comes down to it, the dealer wants to sell as many cars as possible and they will do anything to do it. They are not in the business of keeping cars on the lot. They want them to sell and leave the lot as quickly as possible. Again, don't be fooled by the term "no haggle," it is just another sales tactic that is used in the car business.

GAS VS. HYBRID

The newest type of car out there that everyone wants is a hybrid vehicle. These are cars that have a dual fuel engine. They use gasoline with assistance from electricity. These cars aren't just for tree hugging hippies any more. They not only emit fewer pollutants into the air but will also get good gas mileage. The technology has improved so much over the years that hybrids are now affordable for the general public. This is why with rising fuel costs, people are lining up at the dealership door to purchase a hybrid vehicle just based upon the need to save money on gas. There are waiting lists in a lot of dealerships across the country. Demand is high and supplies are low. Everyone wants to save money on gas. Sounds like a great deal? Not really.

In July of 2003 Popular Mechanics wrote a great story on the comparison between the Honda Civic Hybrid and the Honda Civic EX gas model. The EX model is the higher end of the Civic trim levels and is comparable to the options available in a Civic Hybrid. They drove both vehicles 3065 miles from their New York offices to Southern California to see how each vehicle would do over the long trip. What they found was very interesting. First of all, the hybrid is a more expensive vehicle. Hybrid technology costs more to develop and build. The Civic Hybrid had a sticker price of $20,010 at the time. The Civic EX Gas model had a sticker price of $18,570, a difference of $1440. The window sticker on the hybrid reported that it should get 51 mpg on the highway while the gas model should get 38 mpg. Still sounds good, doesn't it?

Second, what they found was that the actual gas mileage for both was quite different. The hybrid averaged 42 mpg over the trip while the gas model averaged 33.8 mpg. This was lower than advertised but the hybrid still had a 24% better fuel economy over the gas model. This cross country trip required $168 in fuel for the gas model and $135 for the hybrid for a savings of $33. If you divide the $33 over the 3065 miles on the trip, then you have saved about a penny a mile. Looking at this information, **it would take roughly 144,000 miles before the hybrid paid back its $1440 price difference** with the gas model. That is a lot of miles to drive until you actually save money. This difference is even made worse by the fact that most hybrids are sold at sticker price or higher, but the gas models are sold well below sticker price. Therefore, the savings is even less because the price difference is higher. You need even longer to make up the price difference. Even though this report is a few years old, it still rings true as gas mileage and the price difference have changed very little since this report was published.

This does not prove that the dealers are looking to scam people into buying a hybrid. It just shows that your money that you are saving in gas is far outweighed by the difference in price for a hybrid. Gas burning cars are still cheaper to purchase, run and maintain. This may reverse once hybrid technology becomes more cost efficient and brings the price of hybrids down to where they are comparable to gas models. But overall, after doing your research, you may find that what hybrid vehicles advertise on the window sticker as the reported gas mileage may be much higher than you may actually get. They tend to run not as efficiently as advertised. If saving money is not your concern and cutting down on emissions are, then a hybrid may be right for you.

There are other hybrid models out on the market as well. There are several more waiting to be released on the market too. Some are better than others. For example, the Honda Accord hybrid only gets only a few more miles per gallon than its gas burning counterpart yet it costs several thousands of dollars more. There also hybrid SUVs such as the Ford Escape, Lexus RX, and the Toyota Highlander. This is a tough hybrid to develop because, with hybrid technology, you can't get the horsepower or torque needed to use what a lot of SUVs do, such as towing. Plus the mileage difference is not that great and varies depending on driving habits. So the savings really does not exist with some hybrids.

Hybrid cars also run the risk of larger maintenance costs down the road. Your normal everyday backyard mechanic can not work on a hybrid. It requires a lot of special tools and well trained technician to work on it. Any work that needs to be done to the car could be very labor intensive. Therefore, any out of warranty work could be very expensive. These types of cars have not been around long enough to have an established track record for reliability down the road. Nobody really knows if hybrids could have inherent problems down the road.

Keep in mind that at some point your hybrid will end its useful life. You just can't take a hybrid to the junkyard. It has a large battery in it. Have you ever taken a battery to the local dump or transfer station and tried to get rid of it? A battery is considered to be hazardous waste. It has to be handled completely different than normal trash. I personally do not know of any plans by any dealers or junkyards on how to deal with this issue when hybrids come off the road and are no longer useable. Only time will tell.

You also may qualify for a tax credit when you buy a hybrid. It has changed over the years but the IRS usually allows you a tax credit in the year you purchase a hybrid vehicle. This may vary in the future due to the Energy Bill of 2005 that President Bush signed into law. According to the Department of Energy website:

> **"Starting in 2006, hybrid-car buyers and advanced lean-burn technology vehicles will be eligible for tax credits ranging from $1,700-$3,000; this credit is tied with two components: hybrids that save the most fuel compared with 2002 models, and the vehicle's estimated lifetime fuel savings."**

Check with your accountant or the IRS for what you can use for a tax credit. This is a nice way for the government to get the general public to invest in hybrid vehicles but it still isn't a cost effective investment right now even with the tax credit. What many people do not know is there is a downside to this Energy Bill. Once a brand of hybrid models builds a certain amount, the tax credit gets lowered. It keeps going down until the production of hybrid vehicles reaches a level where the tax credit disappears. Since Toyota sells the most amount of hybrid vehicles in the United States, they will be the first one to lose the tax credit. In 2007 they are on track to reach the plateau set forth in the Energy Bill and therefore will no longer have the tax credit. This means the benefit to buying a hybrid gets even smaller.

WHEN IS THE BEST TIME TO BUY?

Believe it or not, some times of the year are better to buy a car than others. Not everyone has the luxury of choosing when they can buy a car. Sometimes cars die, they get in accidents or they get stolen. In that case a car needs to be purchased quickly. But if you have the ability to chose what time of the year to buy your car, then this may help you.

The best time of the year to purchase a car is the week between Christmas and New Years Day. It is the end of the year and the manufacturers want to get their numbers up and finish strong. So they put out some crazy incentives and rebates in order to finish the year strong. A lot of people take that week off of work to spend with family so they have some time to buy a car. A lot of dealers still have leftover vehicles that they need to get rid of. The selection may not be great but the rebates should be big. You could really score a good deal if you shop around. Dealers are very aggressive during this week as they have forecast numbers to attain as well. All the managers want to reach their goals so they can get their bonuses. They do whatever they can to make a deal happen. They even step up their advertising to get more people into the dealership. So they may be more aggressive than normal in trying to earn your business.

The second best time of the year to buy a car is during the week of President's Day. This traditionally a big week for car dealers and they spend lots of money advertising to let everyone know it. It also helps the dealers sell some cars during a slow time of the year. Inventory is usually good, incentives are good and salesmen are hungry for a paycheck. **It's almost a "perfect storm."**

The third best times are holidays in general. Holidays such as July 4th weekend, Memorial Day weekend or Thanksgiving Weekend. These are usually vacation weekends so business is slow. Therefore, the dealer needs to sell cars and will be aggressive in their ability to sell a car. The manufacturer helps them out by giving out good incentives. Sometimes the manufacturer may not even advertise it with the exception of a hard to find place on their website. This is so when the customer gets into the dealership, they can pull out the great incentive, get the customer excited and add a sense of urgency to the situation will cause them to be more likely to buy a car.

If you want to break it down to what time of the month to buy a car, then that would be within the last few days of the month. Car dealers work on a month to month basis. So as the end of the month nears, the dealer wants to push as many deals out the door as they can. The more cars they sell, the more they can earn on the next allocation of cars from the factory. I this case you would need to start your process of buying a car within a few days before the end of the month. Do your test driving in the middle of the month so you are ready to buy by the end of the month.

If you want to break it down to a time of the week to buy a car, then you should buy between Tuesday and Friday in the morning. The reason for this is that those generally are the slower days of the week at the dealer. During the week most customers are working and are not able to shop during the day. So the dealer is generally slow. The morning is good because selling a car is good way to start the day and motivate the troops. A sales manager will work harder to sell a car in the morning because, as the old saying goes, having one in the hand is better than having two in the bush. The saying in the showroom is "motion creates emotion." This means that the more selling that happens, the more others are motivated to work hard and sell more cars. The first sale of the day is usually the best deal. It starts the ball rolling for the rest of the dealership.

Saturdays are one of the worst days to buy a car. It is the busiest day of the week for the dealer so salesman may get busy. They won't have the time to spend with you and give you the quality treatment that you need. They are probably handling 2 to 3 customers at a time and their resources are stretched thin. You may want to try to get a good price, but the salesman may just blow you off since he has other customers in the showroom that may be willing to pay more for the same or a similar car. He doesn't have this luxury during the week when it is much slower.

Don't feel obligated to go shopping at a dealer if they offer a "sale." There actually is no such thing as a "sale" at a car dealer. The word sale just makes you think that you are saving money. It isn't like when Bloomingdales has a sale and everything is 30% off. At the dealer it is just a way of getting people in the door and giving the salesman a chance to make a sale. All the dealers get the same incentives and own their cars for the same amount of money. So a deal you may get at one dealer that is having a "sale" you could also probably get at another dealer that is not advertising one. It is merely a marketing ploy.

THE BAD CAR CYCLE

0% financing, when it went industry wide after 9/11, really threw the car business into a bad cycle of car buying. So many customers purchased cars in the rush of 0% financing when it first came out, that it caused a ripple effect in the supply and demand of cars for years to come. The problem started with the fact that 0% financing brought in so many people and sold so many cars, that when it was all over there were no customers left. Basically, they robbed Peter to pay Paul. They caused customers that were not ready to buy at the time to buy sooner rather than later. **They took tomorrow's customers and made them today's customers.** So for the next six months to a year, most people did not need a new car. They already had one. So after the 0% went away or the dealers ran out of cars, there were very few customers left. The only people who purchased cars purchased them out of necessity.

Before, car sales were relatively steady over time with seasonal fluctuations. Now there are huge peaks and valleys in car sales. Consumers got so comfortable with the "gimmicks" such as 0% or huge rebates that they won't buy a car unless there is a big incentive to. This is when the "Employee Pricing" plan came out.

People came out in droves again to buy cars. So we have another huge peak followed by a deep valley. Hence, the bad car cycle was born. Sales will be flat again until the next gimmick. And to make matters worse the manufacturers are taking a bath with these programs. They are making almost no profit or showing losses. That in turn puts them into financial peril as the domestic manufacturers are in now.

DEALER PAY PLANS

This topic is important because in order to understand how a salesman, Business Manager or Sales Manager works, you need understand how they get paid. How someone gets paid determines how they are motivated and how they try to maximize their pay plan. No two dealers generally have the same pay plan but they usually are very similar.

Salesman, as most people who sell in general, are usually paid a commission on what they sell. Most sales people are paid a small salary with the rest of their pay coming at the end of the month when they get their commission and bonus check. They generally are paid a percentage of the profit made on the vehicle, which ranges from dealer to dealer. Even if a car is sold below invoice, they still get paid. Most dealers have a minimum commission on each car sold. It is usually around $100.

They also have an opportunity to make bonuses. Sometimes they are referred to as "spiffs." A spiff could be an amount of money that is given to the salesman if he sells a certain amount of cars. It sometimes is given out on a daily basis by the Sales Manager. The most common ones that I have seen is something like $100 for the first sale of the day and $300 for a "hat trick" which is selling 3 cars in one day. Spiffs may also be given out to salesman if he sells the oldest car on the lot, or a car that is hard to sell because of the options or color. This is why sometimes a salesman may really try to push you into a certain car that you may not really like. He knows that if he sells it that he could get a nice spiff.

They may also get bonuses at the end of the month for selling the most amounts of cars. This also is why at the end of the month that you could get a good deal because your salesman may be close to reaching a good bonus if he sells one or two more cars. It usually comes down to the last day of the month to see which salesman will be the top salesman and get his bonus. They will be overly aggressive in order to make a deal happen so he can get his bonus.

Sales Managers are paid on commission as well. Their salary may be a little larger than a salesman but their commissions are larger too because they get paid on all of the salesman's deals. They may get spiffs from the dealer as well for reaching goals but the factory may also give them spiffs based upon reaching certain goals as well. They have a lot of opportunity to make extra money this way. But it is all based upon selling cars, lots of them. So like I have said, they are in the business to sell cars, not keep them. As a customer you must remember that you are in a position to make them money so they should know that if they don't sell you a car, no matter what the price, they don't get paid.

Business Managers are paid a little differently. They are paid a small salary but they are paid a good percentage of the other products they sell such as warranties, insurance and the financing. Good Business Managers will work according to their pay plan. Most are paid a higher percentage commission on some products then others while some are paid the same across the board on all products. He may be paid a higher commission on warranties because the dealer wants more warranties to be sold so he can increase his service business.

A good Business Manager will spread his income across the board. He may have 30-50% of his dept. income come from financing with the rest from other products. A weak Business Manager will have 70-90% of the dept. income come from financing. This is because he or she is not good enough to sell any other products. Finance income is the easiest way to make money for a Business Manager. So if he is not good at his job, then you take the easy way out and overcharge your customers on the finance rate. This is bad practice for the long term because eventually the customer will realize they were overcharged on the finance rate. They will be less likely to return to you for repeat business or next time they will get their own financing and will make him no profit the next time around. But again, the Business Manager will do whatever makes him the most amount money. It is always at the expense of the customer.

As you can see by looking at how they get paid, they are all motivated by how they can make the most amount of money. They may come across as your friend, but they really are acting in their best interest, their wallet. Anyone who is paid a commission, no matter what they do, you should be aware of. They will sell you whatever gets them the most amount of money. That is the same in other fields as well such as the jewelry industry, the furniture industry or the insurance industry to name a few.

PROBLEMS WITH THE DEALER AFTER THE SALE

Sometimes after sale is made something goes wrong. This could be something wrong with the car or you realized that the dealer had pulled a fast one with you with the paperwork. No matter what it is, there is recourse. Every state has an Attorney Generals office. Most Attorney Generals office has a division that deals with Consumer Protection or a small group of people that do. They deal with people who were victims of fraud or false advertising.

Over the years, many dealers have been brought up on charges by the Attorney General's office in their state. The charges usually have to do with illegal business practices or false advertising. Some dealers will add things to the car and charge you for it without you knowing it until you look at the paperwork afterwards. They may also tell you that you are financing a car when you really are leasing it. The dealer may also advertise a certain car is for sale but in reality it doesn't exist. This is a "bait and switch" tactic used by the dealer that can get them in trouble if they don't disclose it properly in the ad. Sometimes a dealer will sell you an option that was not in stock at the time of delivery, such as spoiler. The dealer then says that you didn't pay for it and refused to give it you even though the paperwork shows otherwise. There are typical issues that the Attorney General deals with.

The possibilities are endless on what could happen. It could even be as simple as a dealer not fixing a problem found at delivery or shortly thereafter. But regardless, besides holding a survey over their head, as I had mentioned earlier in the book, you can also call the Attorney General in the state that they are in and make a complaint. Usually one call from their office to the dealer will solve the problem. If it doesn't then a remedy is usually recommended to you that may be the best path to take. Sometimes a problem may be covered under the "Lemon Law" statutes of your state as well. Every state has a Lemon Law on the books, but they vary from state to state.

The best way to see what your state has for a Lemon Law is to check out this site that has all of them documented by state: http://autopedia.com/. This site also shows you how to handle the process if you happen to have to go through the Lemon Law. What Lemon Laws were designed for consumers who have purchased cars, new or used, that have inherent mechanical problems that cannot be fixed and so the consumer cannot enjoy the full use of their car. The challenge is to see what the laws are in your state is, when you can make a claim and how you can make a claim. This website should lead you to your state which will show you what protection you do have.

WHAT TO DO AFTER YOU BUY THE CAR

After you buy the car, there are certain things you should do and be aware of. The most obvious thing is to do regular maintenance on your car. This will help you car have less problems as it gets older and will also extend its useful life. A good mileage to get an oil change is every 3000-5000 miles. The more aggressive you drive, the more often you should change your oil. My father always told me that I should change my oil after the first 1000 miles that I drove the car. This was to clean out any metal chips that may have been dislodged after the car left the factory during the break in period. Nowadays there really is not much of a break in period. Each manufacturer is different and you should read the manual to get the actual maintenance requirements for each car. Now it is not always recommended to change your oil within 1000 miles because there is break in oil already in the engine. Changing it prior to 3000 miles may not allow the engine to break itself in with the special oil and will actually damage the engine.

Some car models will have in the manual that no major tune ups are required until 100,000 miles. Some even have it on the window sticker. This can be misconstrued by some people. I knew of a customer who thought "no major tune ups until 100,000 miles" meant no oil changes needed until 100,000 miles. This customer drove the car over 20,000 miles without an oil change even though her engine light was on. Needless to say the engine seized and the car was towed into the dealership. After the customer proceeded to tell us that she never got an oil change because she didn't need to until 100,000 miles. "It's in the manual," she said. Needless to say, she thought her engine was covered by the warranty since it lasted until 36,000 miles. Unfortunately it wasn't covered by the factory warranty because her situation was considered to be abuse by the customer. This customer was devastated but there was nothing we could do to help them. **Just for the record, a major tune up is not an oil change.** It usually entails the changing of spark plugs, timing belt, water pump, air filter, amongst other items recommended by the factory. An oil change may be done at the same time if you are scheduled for one. Please do not make this same mistake. I wouldn't believe it myself if I didn't witness it.

On this note, you do need to do your regularly scheduled maintenance on your vehicle. Your manual usually breaks out what is recommended as far as oil and what needs to be done and when. While this maintenance is recommended, it does not need to be done by the dealer. It may be convenient for it to be done at the dealer since they can keep all the records on file. But it can be cheaper to have it done elsewhere. There are many other car service centers that can do the same recommended services and charge you less. It does not void your factory warranty. Your factory warranty does not require the dealer to do the work, it just requires that it is done. They only request the maintenance information if a warranty claim is made that directly or indirectly involves the work completed during the maintenance. For example, if your engine fails at 15,000 miles, then the factory may want to make sure that you didn't abuse the car and that you did change the oil as recommended.

Your factory warranty is a limited factory warranty. Most consumers think of it as "bumper to bumper." Oddly enough, it does not cover the bumpers. They are considered to be cosmetic and are not covered by warranty. It is a "limited" warranty which means there are limitations. Wear and tear items, cosmetic pieces and normal maintenance are not covered. Items such as tires, brake pads, light bulbs, fabric or leather seats, the muffler and even some seals and gaskets are usually not covered. Items that are defective from the factory are usually covered. For example, if you drive out of the dealership with your new car and 100 feet down the road you drive through a large pothole and bend your rim, you will not be covered. That may be covered under your car insurance, but it will not be covered by your factory warranty. Your factory warranty will cover items that are considered to be a factory defect. Those are items that come from the factory where the car was built and not working properly. Every manufacturer covers different items so you may want to research on the manufacturer's website what is actually covered or not covered. You also should not use your car for anything that it is not designed to do. Driving off road with your sedan, using it as a taxi, competitive racing, altering the exhaust system or adding nitrous oxide are a few things that will void your warranty for most cars. What is not considered to be normal use of your car is usually broken out in the manual as well.

FINAL CHECKLIST

Now you have all the information that is necessary to get a good deal when buying a car. What I have here is a checklist to use for when you go through the whole process. You should make copies of this and keep it with all of your research to see if you are following the process and don't forget anything along the way.

1. Decide on what you need or want

   - 2 or 4 door
   - 2WD or 4WD
   - Color
   - Automatic or manual transmission
   - Leather or cloth
   - What are you using the car for?
   - What options do you need?

2. Do research on your vehicle that you want

   - Consumer Reports
   - Messageboards or blogs
   - Friends and family

3. Find out what you can afford
   - Figure out your budget (monthly payment if you are financing)
   - Check out newspapers for pricing
   - Check your credit scores
   - Figure out a payment
   - Check insurance costs
   - Figure out a purchase price that you can afford (if you are paying cash)

4. Get pre-approved at your local bank or credit union
   - This should determine your interest rate
   - Determine whether you want to take advantage of special financing

5. Test drive the cars you are interested in

6. Determine which car that you want
   - Make a list of 3-4 dealers that you want to visit

7. Visit dealers
   - Bring research paperwork with you
   - Park trade-in out of view
   - Dress casual

8. Get their best "out the door" price
   - Have them document it
   - Break out the sale price and the administrative fees
   - Tell them you will buy from the dealer with the best total price
   - Do not fill out anything they ask. Only give your name and basic info.
   - If you want any other products (warranty, LoJack, etc.) then have them added separately

9. Determine if you want to trade-in your car or sell it
   - Get an average book value on your trade-in

- Don't let the dealer know about your trade until after you get your numbers
- Have them break the numbers out separately from the purchase price
- Don't fill out any questionnaires about your car

10. Layout all the dealer offers
   - Compare sale prices as well as administrative fees
   - Look at the final prices and start calling the dealers
   - Call dealer #2 and ask them to beat dealer #1's price, etc.
   - Keep going until the dealers won't go any lower

11. Have the dealer with the lowest price send you a Purchase & Sale Agrmnt.
   - Check the numbers to make sure they match
   - Make sure it is signed by a manager
   - Make sure your deposit, if you make one, is not a "partial payment"

12. Look over car again to make sure it is the same one you looked at before

13. Visiting the Business Manager
   - Don't fill out any questionnaires
   - Double and triple check the numbers
   - Make him aware that you are financing elsewhere
   - Shop around for prices on any product you choose to buy
   - Some products may be available through your car insurance
   - Be aware of the selling method he uses and how to handle it
   - Make sure the title work is spelled properly and all info is correct
   - Don't let him answer a question
   - Always be on your toes

14. Make sure your car is good condition prior to driving off

15. Make sure everything is OK before filling out the survey
16. Read manual and set up maintenance schedule
17. Enjoy your car
18. Smile! You just saved yourself a whole lot of money on your car!

This checklist should help you in the process of buying a car. The good thing about it is that if you get stuck at any point, you can go back to the chapter and section on that topic and find out what you need in order to make sure you do it right. This may be something that you want to photocopy and use over and over again every time you buy a car.

Now that you know how to buy a car without paying too much, you probably should see the difference of the savings that would happen if you didn't use this book. So you can see what you really are saving. I'll use an average deal as an example.

Car Purchase:		**Profit:**
Purchase Price:	$25,000	$1,500
Trade-in amount:	$8,000	$2,000
Actual Cash Value of trade:	$10,000	
Base Amount Financed (dealer bank):	$17,000	$1,000
Extended Warranty:	$1,500	$700
Life and Disab. Insurance:	$1,000	$350
LoJack:	$795	$300
Total Price:	**$20,295**	**$5850**

So you can see how much profit can be made from a car purchase from someone who was not as knowledgeable as you after reading this book. Here is how it should look after you read this book.

Car Purchase:		Profit:
Purchase Price:	$24,000	$500
Trade-in amount:	$10,000	$0
ACV of trade:	$10,000	
Base Amount Financed (own bank):	$14,000	$0
Extended Warranty:	$900	$100
Life and Disab. Insurance:	$1,000	$350
LoJack:	$595	$100
Total Price:	**$16,495**	**$1050**

As you can see here, in this situation, you could save yourself about $4700 on an average car deal. The dealer makes a fair profit and you get a good deal. Do you now think that your investment in this book was well worth it? You've saved several times over the cost of this book. And that is only on one car purchase. Multiply that by every car purchase that you are going to make over the rest of your life. It can add up to a lot of money over time.

This book can be used as a guide throughout the entire process of buying a car. I've tried to organize this book so you can flip to different sections of this book to help you out with certain areas of the process with ease. The more you go through the process, the easier it will be. What I tried to do is explain why the dealers do some of the things that they do. Because in order to understand what something is sometimes, you need to understand why they do it. The motivation of a car dealer, manager or salesman is the driving force of how a customer is handled and whether or not he or she gets a good deal.

Hopefully you have enjoyed reading this as much as I enjoyed writing it. This should change the way you buy cars for the rest of your life. Please share it with others so everyone has an opportunity to save a ton of money whenever they buy a car.

GLOSSARY OF TERMS

ACV – Actual Cash Value. This is the true value of the car that you are trading in.

ADM – Additional Dealer Markup. Markup that is added to a high demand vehicle above and beyond the MSRP.

Administration fees – Additional fees above and beyond the sale price that each dealer charges in order to process the paperwork.

Advance – The percentage of invoice or book value that a bank will loan a customer depending on their credit.

APR – Annual Percentage Rate. It is your interest rate on your finance contract.

Back End profit – The profit a dealer makes from all the other products sold on the car such as financing, warranties, insurance, alarms, etc.

Balloon note – A method of purchase where at the end of a specific term, a large lump sum payment of the balance is due.

Bank draft – A type of payment given to a customer to pay for a car at a dealership. It is designed to only pay for a car under the conditions set forth by the bank. Also called a "Draft Note."

Bump – When a salesman gets to agree to a higher payment than you originally wanted.

Buy rate – The interest rate that a dealer buys money from the bank on a finance contract.

Buyers Order – A legal document between a customer and the dealer showing the vehicle to be purchased, the price agreed upon and the name of the buyer and seller. Also known as a Purchase and Sale Agreement.

Cherry picking – When a salesman looks at all of the customers on the lot and approaches the one that looks like the easiest sale based upon how they look.

Dealer cash – An amount given to the dealer by the factory in order to help sell more cars by means of competitive pricing in addition to holdback and advertising.

Deductible – The amount of money the customer is responsible for on each warranty claim.

Demo unit – Demonstrator Unit. This is a new car that is used by a dealership and then sold after a few thousand miles. It is still treated as a new car in the factory's eyes.

Deposit – An amount of money that is given to the dealer to hold a car you are purchasing. It should be given back if the deal falls through.

Depreciation – The value that your car loses over time.

Devaluing your car – The act of when a dealer walks around your trade-in and points out every little defect in order to make you think that your car is worth less than it really is.

Draft note – See "Bank Draft."

Factory Survey – The survey that you receive, either by mail or by phone, that lets the factory know how the dealer is treating their customers.

FICO – Fair Isaac Corp. This organization figures your credit score for all three credit bureaus.

Finance Reserve – The amount of money made by the dealer from marking up the finance rate on the customers finance contract.

Floorplan – A credit line held by a dealer in order to purchase their inventory from the factory.

Floorplan credits – When a dealer sells a unit from their inventory before their free floorplan days are up. This goes back to the dealer each billing period.

Front end profit – The profit a dealer makes on the car itself when it is sold.

Holdback – A percentage of the value of a car that the factory holds back until the car is sold. It is paid to the dealer every quarter.

Hybrid – A dual fuel vehicle. It is usually powered by gasoline and electricity.

Marketing incentives – An amount of money given to the dealer in order to sell more cars by more advertising in addition to holdback or dealer cash.

Mental ownership – When a customer already feels like they own the car that they are looking at.

Money Factor – The factor used when figuring most leases. It is a small number, such as .00239, that can be translated into an interest rate by multiplying it by 2400.

MSRP – Manufacturers Suggested Retail Price. It is the price on the window sticker of new cars.

Negative Equity – When you owe more on your car than it is worth. Ex.: Trade-in is worth $5,000 but you owe $7,000. Your negative equity is $2,000. Also known as "Upside Down."

No haggle – A pricing strategy used by certain dealers. It is when one price is placed on a car and it is non-negotiable. Also called a "One Price Store."

One price store – See "No Haggle."

Packed payment – A payment that is quoted to a customer that has several products added to it as well as the base car payment without the knowledge of the customer.

Partial Payment – An amount of money given to a dealer as a form of payment towards the balance on a vehicle. Definition may vary from state to state.

PDI – Pre-Delivery Inspection. The process a car goes through by the service dept. before it is delivered.

Purchase and Sale Agreement – See Buyers Order.

Residual Value – The percentage of the MSRP that the bank sets as the value of your car at the end of the lease.

Rust and Dust – The dealer name for paint and fabric protection that they try to sell.

Sell rate – The interest rate that a dealer sells money from the bank to the customer on a finance contract.

Special Financing – Low finance rates that are sponsored by the factory for a certain model of car. Also known as subvented finance rates.

Spiffs – Bonuses given to a salesman or manager based upon his performance or if he reaches special goals.

Spot Delivery – When a customer takes delivery of their car the same day that they agree on the sale.

Sub-prime credit – A term used to describe customers whose credit does not qualify for the best credit programs. Can also be called "Non-prime credit."

Subvented financing – See Special Financing.

SUV – Sport Utility Vehicle.

Swapping – When a dealer swaps a car from their inventory with a similar car from another dealer.

Teaser payment – A marketing term where a low payment, that is only attainable under the perfect conditions, is used in an advertisement to get customers into the dealership.

Theft Deterrent Device – A device that deters a car from being stolen. Example: Audible alarm, the "Club", kill switches, etc.

Theft Recovery Device – A device that helps a car get recovered once it is stolen. It is not activated until the car is stolen.

Third Party Warranty – A warranty that is issued by a company other than the factory.

Trade Difference – A misleading method of how a dealer gives you the value of your trade. They subtract the value of the trade from the sale price to give you a "trade difference."

Upside Down – See "Negative Equity."

VSI – Vendors Single Interest. A fee charged by most banks. It is a small insurance policy on each customer that pays the bank if the car is to be repossessed and it is nowhere to be found.

BRIAN'S RECOMMENDED WEBSITES

Automobilemag.com – Automobile Magazine - The official Automobile Magazine Website features news, road tests, a complete car buying and leasing guide, live auto show coverage, and much more.

Autopedia.com – A website that is an encyclopedia on a large amount of information on cars including Lemon Laws.

CapitalOne.com – Capital One Auto Finance – A source of financing for consumers with all types of credit, specializes in sub-prime financing.

CarandDriver.com – Car and Driver magazine - Car and Driver Online provides the most comprehensive source of automotive reviews and comparison information.

Cars.com – A website that gives out pricing and other information for cars and allows you to buy or sell cars.

CarTalk.com – A talk show on NPR (National Public Radio) about cars and related topics.

CNA.com - A third party warranty provider that has been in business since 1897 supplying warranty coverage to both new and used cars.

ConsumerReports.org – Consumer Reports magazine – A magazine that rates all types of consumer products including cars. They do not accept advertising.

CuDirect.com – Credit Union Direct Lending – An online credit union car finance website that gives access to thousands of credit unions across the country.

Edmunds.com - A great website for finding the invoice prices or new cars, rebates, marketing incentives or dealer cash as well as used car values.

ELoan.com – A source of online auto financing.

FreeCreditReport.com – A website that allows you to get a free copy of your credit report once a year.

Galves.com – Publisher of a used car pricing guide.

Household Auto Finance (HSBC) - **http://www.hsbcusa-autoloans.com/ CarLoans/FrontPage.jst** - A source of auto financing for consumers with all types of credit, specializes in sub-prime financing.

KBB.com - Kelley Blue Book – Publisher of a used car pricing guide used mainly on the West Coast.

LeaseTrader.com - A website designed to help customers get out of their lease by having qualified customers take over their lease.

MotorTrend.com - Official Motor Trend magazine web site features used cars, road tests, new cars, concept cars, auto shows, and much more car buying information and help.

NADA.com – National Automobile Dealer Association – Publisher of one of the most popular used car guides.

NHTSA.gov – National Highway Traffic and Safety Administration – A government agency that tracks safety and recall records. Has reports and studies on transportation related topics such as odometer fraud, safety belt use, child safety, crash tests, etc.

RoadandTrack.com – Road and Track Magazine - America's oldest automotive enthusiast magazine

SwapaLease.com – A website designed to help customers get out of their lease by having qualified customers take over their lease.

Zurichna.com/zdu – Zurich is a third party warranty provider, formerly known as Universal Underwriters, that has been in business since 1922 supplying warranty service to new and used cars.

BONUS

Go to www.CarBuyingRevealed.com to find added bonuses available to you. You will find worksheets for detailing the whole process of getting the best price as well as an added bonus of the "The Top 50 Ways Mechanics Recommend to Increase the Life of Your Automobile." All of this is available for you to download for free! You just need to visit www.CarBuyingRevealed.com in order to get it.

These worksheets will help you maximize your potential for saving the most amount of money when going through the process of buying your car. Start saving money now by downloading these worksheets!

Don't forget to download the "The Top 50 Ways Mechanics Recommend to Increase the Life of Your Automobile." This will help you save money during the life of your car by simply following what the people who work on your car have learned over the years from personal experience.

Now go out there at save yourself some money!

LaVergne, TN USA
03 February 2011
215151LV00002B/43/P